Beginning

Introducing the Good News of the Kingdom of God
and the Name of Jesus Christ

Volume 1

Acknowledgments: Thank you to Tom Graham and Jim Styles for their suggestions and feedback on the manuscript. Thank you also to Pat Hampson for her proofreading.

Cover Design: Jason Robinson 2019

Published in the United States of America 2019

ISBN: 9781091695566

Each chapter from this book was originally a blog post from thisisyourbible.com

Preface

The gospel should make sense.

It is God's message of hope to the world. It is simple, yet profound: He will fill the earth with His glory (Numbers 14:21).

But unfortunately, sometimes we read passages, or we hear the Bible expounded, and what we hear simply *doesn't* make sense. Sometimes, we feel as though the answers we are given tend to create even more questions.

This book has been written to take some of the divine principles and truths expressed in the Bible and to convey them clearly and easily to the reader. In doing so, the hope is that the logic, simplicity, and yet power of the gospel will be evident.

Each chapter is only two to four pages long. It can be read in just a few minutes, and thus become part of a daily routine—a way that you can start the day with a positive thought, or end the day with good news.

Throughout the Acts of the Apostles, Christians went from town to town, preaching the gospel—as Jesus had commanded them to do (Mark 16:15). That gospel is neatly summarized in Philip's preaching to the Samaritans: "he preached good news about the kingdom of God and the name of Jesus Christ" (Acts 8:12). The gospel, or the good news, is effectively comprised of two parts—the things of the kingdom of God and the name of Jesus Christ. This book is divided into two sections, following that division.

The chapters originally appeared as blog posts on www.thisisyourbible.com. The website's purpose is the same as this book: to present the gospel in a clear and concise way. If you would like to know more about the Bible, you will find numerous resources there.

May you find these pages inspiring and motivating. May they encourage you to ask questions, and also help you to find answers.

Jason Hensley
2019

Table of Contents

Part I

The Good News
of the Kingdom of God

Section I
The Basics of the Kingdom

Chapter I - Something Much Better

Sometimes life is hard.

In fact, it can be hard more than just sometimes. When we have exams due or when we have a large project to finish at work, or when we've just had one of those "difficult conversations" with someone, life is hard. When unforeseen circumstances come into our lives, or the lives of those whom we love, life is hard. Sometimes we feel broken. Sometimes we feel shattered. Sometimes we just place our head in our hands and cry.

And yet, despite life's anxieties and its frustrations, it doesn't always have to be difficult—or even more, the God of Scripture promises that there is a time coming when it won't *ever* be difficult. Just consider what the apostle Paul wrote to the Christians in Corinth:

"We are afflicted in every way, but not crushed; perplexed, but not driven to despair; persecuted, but not forsaken; struck down, but not destroyed." 2 Corinthians 4:8-9

The apostle had a difficult life. Later, in that same letter, he listed off some of the things that he had to endure—which included beatings, scourgings, and being stoned (2 Corinthians 11:23-28)! When he wrote to the brethren, he could honestly say "we are afflicted in every way." But at the same time, though he could write to them about all of these difficulties, he ended each of his descriptions of persecution with a ray of hope—they were afflicted in every way possible, but they were not crushed. They were perplexed and confused, but they were not in despair. They were persecuted and physically injured, but they knew that they were not forsaken. People had even gone to the point of striking them—but the apostle could confidently say that they had not been destroyed.

It's an astonishing admission from the apostle—though he and his friends had gone through the fire, they had not been crushed. Later in his life, when Paul was looking death straight in the eye, he continued to express this same outlook:

"Then Paul answered, 'What are you doing, weeping and breaking my heart? For I am ready not only to be imprisoned but even to die in Jerusalem for the name of the Lord Jesus.'" Acts 21:13

At this point in his life, the apostle Paul knew that dangers awaited him at Jerusalem—yet regardless, he declared that he was wholly devoted to his Lord. He was willing, not only to be imprisoned, but also to die at Jerusalem.

It's an astonishing outlook on life—and at a certain point, it can almost sound foolhardy. It would almost seem as though Paul simply didn't care about life or

2

thought that his life was meaningless. Nevertheless, such wasn't the case. In fact, looking back at what he wrote to the Christians in Corinth, he actually explained *why* he was able to have this outlook on life. It wasn't indifference or apathy towards life that caused him to feel this way. It wasn't a rashness or irresponsibility. It wasn't depression. Instead, it was totally the opposite—despite what he may have had to suffer, the apostle felt *empowered* because he had a hope for a time when *suffering would be eradicated*:

"For this light momentary affliction is preparing for us an eternal weight of glory beyond all comparison, as we look not to the things that are seen but to the things that are unseen. For the things that are seen are transient, but the things that are unseen are eternal." 2 Corinthians 4:17-18

When the apostle suffered, he knew that the suffering was preparing him for something glorious. Though the whip stung upon his back, he knew that the pain and the frustrations that he endured in this life couldn't be compared with the glory that he would be given, by God's grace, in the future. Again, he said the same thing to the Christians in Rome:

"For I reckon that the sufferings of this present time are not worthy to be compared with the glory which shall be revealed in us." Romans 8:18 KJV

The apostle's belief in the future was so strong that he felt as though all of his suffering *couldn't even be compared* to the glory that would be given to him by the Father! The future age was beautiful, and the apostle's vision of that future time could bring him through anything—causing him to proclaim that he was even willing to die for his Lord Jesus.

Just imagine how our lives—those lives which are sometimes filled with similar frustrations and sufferings—could be changed if we could think like the apostle. Just image how stressful situations could be transformed if we could look to the glory of the future.

And so, that's what we'll attempt to do in the next few chapters. We'll comb through the prophecies of the future and through the promises of God, and in doing so, we'll seek to understand what it was that the apostle found so empowering about the future— and we'll attempt to make that hope our own.

Chapter 2 - Life from Death

No matter what happened, the apostle Paul asserted that all of this life's suffering wasn't even worthy to be compared with what was to come (Romans 8:18 KJV). In all of his frustrations and even his pain, he could look past that time to something better—something that he called "the glory which shall be revealed in us." That glory was so great that even the afflictions that he suffered paled in comparison to it—they weren't even *worthy* to be compared!

But what was that "glory" to which he looked forward? And what did he mean by it being revealed "in us"?

In looking at his epistles, we see that he uses this same idea time and again—and in looking at some of these passages, that glory and that hope which he cherished becomes readily apparent. Just consider some of these passages:

"But our citizenship is in heaven, and from it we await a Savior, the Lord Jesus Christ, who will transform our lowly body to be like his glorious body, by the power that enables him even to subject all things to himself." Philippians 3:20-21

This is the hope upon which the apostle waited. This was the glory. Someday, his "lowly body" would be made like the Lord's "glorious body"—he would be changed from mortal to immortal, like the Lord Jesus (1 Corinthians 15:42-43)! It would be changed to a body that would never sin (Romans 6:23)! This was the transformation that would take place on the believers—this was the glory that would be revealed in them!

In one of his last epistles, the apostle talked about the same thing, but this time, he explained *when* it would happen:

"When Christ who is your life appears, then you also will appear with him in glory." Colossians 3:4

Once again, the believers would appear *in glory*— they would be given immortality—yet this time, he gave some extra information: the believers would be "in glory" when Christ appeared! It would take place at his second coming! Again, when writing to the Thessalonians, he affirmed this idea and connected it with another:

"We exhorted each one of you and encouraged you and charged you to walk in a manner worthy of God, who calls you into his own kingdom and glory." 1 Thessalonians 2:12

This glory, this immortality, would come at the same time that the Lord Jesus returned to the earth to bring about his kingdom. They had been called to God's "kingdom and glory"—as though the two terms were intimately connected.

Indeed, what a hope it was that the apostle had! Just imagine life out of death! Imagine life without the pain that comes from sin! Imagine life without the temptation to do evil! Though life could crush him, he could always look past the bitter times and remember that by God's grace, there would be a day when the Lord Jesus would return. When he returned, he would establish a kingdom, and he would give true, sinless and endless life to his followers.

But, really, that's just the tip of the iceberg.

Chapter 3 - A Perfect King

What if politicians never lied?

What if you could have absolute faith in everything that the government ever said?

What if you could believe every word and every promise that the president or the prime minister of your country said to you?

Then perhaps it could be said that you had entered into the kingdom of God.

Every kingdom has a king, or some type of ruler. The kingdom of God is no exception—except that its ruler is no ordinary man or woman: it's the Lord Jesus Christ. Just before the Lord was born, the angel Gabriel declared his role:

"And behold, you will conceive in your womb and bear a son, and you shall call his name Jesus. He will be great and will be called the Son of the Most High. And the Lord God will give to him the throne of his father David, and he will reign over the house of Jacob forever, and of his kingdom there will be no end." Luke 1:31-33

Jesus was destined to be the king over God's kingdom. He would rule, sitting on the throne of David, the first righteous king of Israel, and thus, would rule from the city of Jerusalem, the place where David set up his throne (2 Samuel 5:6, 9; Jeremiah 3:17).

And yet, though he will sit upon David's throne, his kingdom will be much greater than David's ever was —and one of the reasons for this superlative greatness is the king himself.

Just try to imagine what it will be like to live in a nation where the Lord Jesus is the King—where the King is someone who is sinless (1 Peter 2:22), someone who knows the thoughts of those around him (Mark 2:8), someone who has all power in heaven and earth (Matthew 28:18), and someone who speaks God's words (John 14:24). You'd never have to wonder about anything that he said—it would always be true. You'd never have to wonder about any of his motives—they would always be pure. You'd never have to second-guess any of his decisions—they would always be absolutely right. You could put total trust and total faith in everything that he did!

The prophet Isaiah actually gives us a picture of this whole scenario:

"There shall come forth a shoot from the stump of Jesse, and a branch from his roots shall bear fruit. And the Spirit of the LORD shall rest upon him...And his delight shall be in the fear of the LORD. He shall not judge by what his eyes see, or decide disputes by what his ears hear, but with righteousness he shall judge the poor." Isaiah 11:1-4

It isn't always corruption that causes people and human governments to make wrong choices. Sometimes they simply don't have all of the information they need to make the best choice. In a court of law, all of the evidence isn't always available or isn't always conclusive.

But not so in the Lord's government. The Lord Jesus, the one who is descended from David and who will sit on David's throne, will be filled with the spirit of God and will judge with righteousness and equity. He won't judge with the sight of his eyes—he won't need to. He'll know immediately what is right and what is wrong! Conflicts will be judged justly. Decisions will be made perfectly.

What a change from today. In a world where so much time is spent deliberating and so much ink is spilled arguing over policies and politics, it's hard to imagine anything different.

But perhaps the most beautiful thing about all of this is that someday, it *will* be different—the kingdom of God isn't simply a daydream or some pretty story. It's real. It's going to happen. Someday, the corruption that plagues every government, that plagues all human leadership, will be done away. In its place will be the throne of David—and sitting on that throne will be the one who judges in righteousness and in truth.

Even so, come Lord Jesus.

Chapter 4 - Elusive Peace

Lately, it seems as though most of the international news is tragic. With the war that went on in Israel and its effects on the people of Gaza, the situation in Ukraine, and all of the problems connected to the rise of the Islamic State, it could feel as though the world is falling apart. One tragedy happens after another—and as a result, daddy doesn't come home one night, little brother or sister is put into a sleep from which they will never wake up, and the family is changed forever.

It's a hardened and stubborn man who isn't moved by the events that have happened in the last few months and by their impact on those who have had to suffer through them.

And yet, for those of us who have heard about the kingdom of God, it just makes us long for that time even more.

Because it won't always be this way.

In the last chapter, we saw who will be king in the kingdom of God: the Lord Jesus Christ. As a man who has never sinned and as a man who has all power in heaven and in earth (Matthew 28:18), he will be the perfect ruler. Unlike many rulers who have used their power to oppress the people, the Lord will be a very different type of king. Certainly, everyone will need to submit to him (Isaiah 60:12). Yet, the result of his rulership will be something that the world has never seen—something which it has constantly sought to attain, yet something which has repeatedly proved to be quite elusive:

"They shall not hurt or destroy in all my holy mountain; for the earth shall be full of the knowledge of the LORD as the waters cover the sea." Isaiah 11:9

We saw in the last chapter that this passage was about Christ and what he would do. With that in mind, we see that part of his kingdom will be this everlasting peace—no one will "hurt" or "destroy"! As it sounds, war will be eradicated and a perfect peace will settle over God's "holy mountain," or Mount Zion. Israel will have quietness. No more torn families. No more children crying over their parents.

Yet, this perfect peace will not just be in Israel. It will settle over the entirety of the globe! Just let the power of these words sink in as you read them:

"He shall judge between many peoples, and shall decide for strong nations far away; and they shall beat their swords into plowshares, and their spears into pruning hooks; nation shall not lift up sword against nation, neither shall they learn war anymore." Micah 4:3

This is what the Lord Jesus will do—we know that because the context of this verse is all about the "latter days" (v. 1) and a time in which the nations of the world will want to know more about God's way and His truth (v. 2). Thus, the Lord will be the one who judges between the nations, and with his perfectly righteous and true judgments, all conflicts will be settled. War will be a thing of the past. In fact, it will be so foreign to people that all of those weapons which they once had, their "swords" and their "spears" will be turned into things like "plowshares" and "pruning hooks." Firearms, missiles, bombs, and all of their counterparts will be so useless that people will try to think of ways that they can salvage the material!

That peace which has been so elusive, that peace which has been the aim of the United Nations for years, will finally come to pass. Yet, it won't come about as the result of man's actions. It won't be because the nations have, of their own volition, decided to work together. Instead, it will be the result of a righteous king, ruling upon the throne of David, and judging with perfect judgment.

May that day come quickly—so that the tragedy that engulfs this world will be transformed into peace.

Chapter 5 - Conflicting Views

If you were to take a survey of most of Christianity about life after death, what do you think you would learn? What if you were to ask specifically about what took place to *believers* after they died? And then, even more, not just what happened to them, but what they spent eternity doing?

What do you think most people would say?

Many of us are taught about this long before we were ever able to read. We learned about it in Sunday school, or we heard it from one of our parents when a relative or friend passed away. We heard phrases like "well, he's just looking down on us now."

For centuries, the idea of heaven-going has been ingrained in our culture. To "send" someone off to heaven at their death is a socially permissible—perhaps even a socially required—thing to do. If we don't, then what does it mean about that person?

And yet, if we were ever challenged to describe the afterlife, or paint a picture of heaven, few of us really could—if we could get beyond the stereotypical "sitting on clouds with harps" scene. Our understanding of life after death doesn't often go far beyond what we're taught when we are young.

With that in mind, think about what we have considered in these past articles—and remember the detail that Scripture gives:

1. The apostle Paul had hope beyond this life.
2. His hope lay in the resurrection from the dead.
3. At that time, Jesus will rule in perfection from David's throne.
4. And peace will finally be brought to this stricken world.

Just consider those four points in light of what our culture so often dictates about life after death—and, oddly enough when we try to match it up with the points that we've seen in Scripture, the two just don't quite go together.

How was it that the apostle, when thinking about hope beyond our current plight, looked to the time of the *resurrection* (1 Corinthians 15:12-14, 43), and not the time of his ascension to heaven? Wouldn't his hope of life and peace be found in his picture of life in the clouds? Why is it that Jesus is said to rule on the "throne of David" (Luke 1:32), when David's throne was in *Jerusalem?* Why does Scripture discuss the prospect of *peace on earth* and yet we so often discuss peace beyond the skies?

Something just doesn't fit. It's almost as though the Scriptures put forth this idea that death is very different than our society has so often pictured it. Rather than being something in which our "souls" continue on, it's a type of "sleep" (1 Corinthians 15:18; 1 Thessalonians 4:13-15). Then, once the Lord Jesus returns, the resurrection occurs (1 Thessalonians 4:16), the bodies of the faithful are changed and glorified (Colossians 3:4), and the kingdom of God—the rule of Jesus Christ—comes over the earth.

In fact, over and over, it was this hope of the kingdom to come that the Lord Jesus consistently emphasized to his disciples. This was a crucial part of their faith. It wasn't finding a place on a cloud in heaven, and perhaps that's why our vision of heaven is often so blurry—it might not be the hope emphasized in the Word of God. Instead, Scripture focuses on this kingdom. Just notice some of Christ's words—it's even in what we call "the Lord's prayer":

""Our Father in heaven, hallowed be your name. Your kingdom come, your will be done, on earth as it is in heaven." Matthew 6:9-10

In the very first words of his well-known prayer, the Lord told his disciples to pray and long for the kingdom—something which would eventually come on *this earth*. Just a few chapters later, he showed them once again that this was the hope of the faithful:

""When the Son of Man comes in his glory, and all the angels with him, then he will sit on his glorious throne. Before him will be gathered all the nations, and he will separate people one from another as a shepherd separates the sheep from the goats. And he will place the sheep on his right, but the goats on the left. Then the King will say to those on his right, 'Come, you who are blessed by my Father, inherit the kingdom prepared for you from the foundation of the world." Matthew 25:31-34

Though society focuses on this idea of heaven-going, Scripture seems to have a different emphasis. Instead, the Lord's disciples hoped to hear the words, "Come, you who are blessed by my Father, inherit the kingdom prepared for you from the foundation of the world."

And, if that was their hope, can we really be wrong in thinking that it should be ours?

Chapter 6 - The Hope of Israel

So far in our consideration of the kingdom of God, we have seen a number of its different aspects. We have seen that it will come when the Lord Jesus returns and raises the dead. We have seen that it will be a time of peace on the earth. We have seen that it will be a time in which Jesus rules as a divine and perfect monarch. We have seen that it, instead of heaven-going, was the hope of the apostles. Yet, there is one major aspect of it upon which we have not yet touched. Just notice the term that the apostle Paul used when referring to his hope:

"For this reason, therefore, I have asked to see you and speak with you, since it is because of the hope of Israel that I am wearing this chain." Acts 28:20

When talking to the Jews in Rome, the apostle Paul defined his hope as "the hope of Israel." It's an intriguing statement, because it's not something that we often associate with Christianity. Christianity came out of Judaism, so it seems almost out of place to say that a Christian's hope is the "hope of Israel." But what did the apostle mean?

Though they may not be that well known today, there is a set of promises that God made to a man named Abraham, the father of the Jewish people. In those promises, God detailed that he would bless Abraham, make his descendants a great nation, and give them the land of Canaan (Genesis 12:1-3). Even more, all of the world would be eventually be blessed by

Abraham's descendants (Genesis 22:18)—and by one descendant in particular (Galatians 3:16). By the time that Abraham died, these promises had not yet been fulfilled (Hebrews 11:13). Thus, knowing that God would eventually do what He had promised, the people of Israel fervently waited to see their fulfillment. We see this attitude reflected in the word of King David:

"Remember his covenant forever, the word that he commanded, for a thousand generations, the covenant that he made with Abraham, his sworn promise to Isaac, which he confirmed to Jacob as a statute, to Israel as an everlasting covenant, saying, 'To you I will give the land of Canaan, as your portion for an inheritance.'" 1 Chronicles 16:15-18

They were to "remember his covenant forever." These promises were essential to keep in mind. They were the basis of the future for Israel—they proclaimed a blessing upon the whole world! As such, these promises became "the hope" of the people of Israel and became a formative part of their faith. Thus, even in the time just before the Lord's birth, the Jews were thinking about these promises. Just consider what Mary, the mother of the Lord Jesus, said before Christ was born:

"He has helped his servant Israel, in remembrance of his mercy, as he spoke to our fathers, to Abraham and to his offspring forever." Luke 1:54-55

In the promise of the Lord Jesus, Mary saw a reference to the promises to Abraham! That covenant had become part of her hope! Along the same lines, notice what Zacharias, the father of John the Baptist, said just after John was born:

"And has raised up a horn of salvation for us in the house of his servant David...to remember his holy covenant, the oath that he swore to our father Abraham, to grant us that we, being delivered from the hand of our enemies, might serve him without fear." Luke 1:69, 72-74

As the process for the Messiah's birth was put into place, Zacharias saw the fulfillment of the promises to Abraham. And it filled him with joy—because these promises were the hope of the people of Israel! Therefore, when the apostle Paul stated that his hope was "the hope of Israel," it would seem as though he was stating that his hope for the future was bound up in the promises made to Abraham.

Sadly, as we saw in the last chapter, often the hope of the apostles, the kingdom of God, is obscured by the teaching of heaven-going. Perhaps one of the reasons why this has taken place is the slow-but-steady neglect of these promises and the "hope of Israel."

And so, if we really want to understand the kingdom of God and the hope of the apostles, it behooves us to spend time trying to understand these promises.

Section 2
The Promises to Abraham

Chapter 7 - Unbreakable Promises

Have you ever made a promise that was too difficult for you to keep? Maybe you promised that you would be somewhere, and then realize that you had a conflicting appointment. Maybe you promised that you would finish a project for work, but you just didn't have the energy or the time to finish it. Whatever the situation was, we've all had that experience—we make mistakes. Unlike us, however, that isn't the case with God. When God makes a promise, He will do it—no matter what.

In our last chapter we looked at the idea of "the hope of Israel," and we saw how this hope was connected to a set of promises that were made to Abraham. In these next few paragraphs, we'll explore those promises and ponder their unbreakableness.

Abraham lived in Ur (Genesis 15:7), which appears to have been a pagan city—and so Abraham would have grown up worshiping false gods (Joshua 24:15). While in this false worship, the true God appeared to Abraham, and told him that he had a plan for him— and he wanted him to leave everything from his old life and go to a land that He would show to him. Upon following that command, He would do mighty things for him:

"Now the Lord said to Abram, "Go from your country and your kindred and your father's house to the land that I will show you. And I will make of you a great nation, and I will bless you and make your name great, so that you will be a blessing. I will bless those who bless you, and him who dishonors you I will curse, and in you all the families of the earth shall be blessed." Genesis 12:1-3

Just imagine if God promised these types of things to you—the One who created the universe, who gives breath to all living things, promised to make these things happen to you and to your descendants! What a gift! A great nation would come from him, he would be blessed and his name would be great, and those who blessed him would be blessed! Even more, in the next chapter of Genesis, God expanded these promises—adding a provision about the land:

"The Lord said to Abram...'Lift up your eyes and look from the place where you are, northward and southward and eastward and westward, for all the land that you see I will give to you and to your offspring forever." Genesis 13:14-15

Abraham would be given all of the land that he could see. And so, throughout Abraham's life, all of these things began to come to pass. He had many children, and saw some of their descendants. He saw his household become great, and filled with many people. And yet, in his old age, when his wife Sarah died, something was still missing:

"And Sarah died at Kiriath-arba (that is, Hebron) in the land of Canaan...And Abraham rose up from before his dead and said to the Hittites, 'I am a sojourner and foreigner among you; give me property among you for a burying place.'" Genesis 23:2-4

Did you notice what just happened? Sarah died, and Abraham was not able to simply bury her! Why? Couldn't he just bury her on their property, as most people did during those times? No! Because, as he said, he was a "sojourner and foreigner"—he didn't own any property! What a strange thing for the one to whom the whole land was promised!

Oddly enough, this lack of property continued even to Abraham's death. When Abraham died, he still did not own any land, except for that upon which he buried Sarah (Acts 7:5). And yet, hadn't God promised him all of the land he could see? What happened?

We know that God keeps his promises. Unlike us, He doesn't get overwhelmed, and He doesn't forget what He has said. If God has promised, then it is as good as done. And so, why was it that God promised the land to Abraham, and yet never gave it to him?

Chapter 8 - God's Timetable

"I promise."

It's a powerful pair of words. They signify absolute commitment, absolute surety, and, as far as you can offer, absolute confidence that what you are saying is going to take place.

As we saw in the last chapter, throughout time, God Himself has made promises. Unlike our promises, which can only be guaranteed inasmuch as we have control over a situation, God's promises will always be kept.

And yet, where we left off last time, God had made a promise, but it hadn't been fulfilled. Many millennia ago, Yahweh had promised Abraham that He would give him all of the land on which he trod (Genesis 13:17). But, when Abraham died, his entire estate was merely composed of a tiny piece of property—just one on which he was able to bury his wife (Genesis 23:17-18). Even more, in that very event where Abraham purchased that burial ground, notice how he described himself:

"I am a sojourner and foreigner among you; give me property among you for a burying place, that I may bury my dead out of my sight." Genesis 23:4

Abraham saw himself as a "sojourner" and a "foreigner." He wasn't a citizen of their country. He didn't have a home there. He was a pilgrim—not in the sense that the word is typically used today, but in the sense of having no permanent territory. He moved around from place to place—because he didn't have any property.

While this might seem unimportant, this sojourner characteristic of Abraham is one that Scripture tends to emphasize. As Stephen spoke before a group of Pharisees and Sadducees, this was a point that he brought up:

"Then he went out from the land of the Chaldeans and lived in Haran. And after his father died, God removed him from there into this land in which you are now living. Yet he gave him no inheritance in it, not even a foot's length, but promised to give it to him as a possession and to his offspring after him, though he had no child." Acts 7:4-5

God promised the land to Abraham, but, at least before he had a child, never even gave him a foot of it! In the epistle to the Hebrews, Abraham's lack of land appears again:

"By faith he went to live in the land of promise, as in a foreign land, living in tents with Isaac and Jacob, heirs with him of the same promise." Hebrews 11:9

Did you notice where Abraham lived? He lived in the land of promise—the place which God had promised to him—and yet, when he lived there, the apostle wrote that he lived *in tents!* A tent wasn't the place of one who owned land! A tent was the dwelling of someone who *moved*, it was the dwelling of a *sojourner*. Indeed, when the writer went on to describe Abraham, he used a very similar word:

"These all died in faith, not having received the things promised, but having seen them and greeted them from afar, and having acknowledged that they were strangers and exiles on the earth." Hebrews 11:13-14

Abraham and his family were "strangers and exiles" on the earth. They didn't ever receive the land that was promised to them—and Scripture seems to make a point of this. But why? Why would God's book go to such lengths to show that God *didn't keep* His promise?

The same apostle went on to answer our question:

"And all these, though commended through their faith, did not receive what was promised, since God had provided something better for us, that apart from us they should not be made perfect." Hebrews 11:39-40

None of the people who were listed in Hebrews 11—all of Abraham's descendants—received the promise. They never fully received the land. Why? "That apart from us they should not be made perfect."

Somehow, it was for us. Somehow, it was so that they would be made perfect at the same time as us. But what does that really mean?

Chapter 9 - Perfection

Perfection.

It's a word that speaks to the unattainable, and yet ultimate goal of most of humanity. For centuries, mankind has sought *perfection*. They have sought perfection in their lives overall, they have sought perfection in their work, and they have sought perfection in both their children and their families.

And yet, for all of that seeking, there's only *ever* been one man who has ever attained it. In considering the Lord Jesus Christ, the writer to the Hebrews wrote:

"Although he was a son, he learned obedience through what he suffered. And being made perfect, he became the source of eternal salvation to all who obey him." Hebrews 5:8-9

Christ, being a son, *learned* to be obedient to God through the things which he suffered. And thus, in learning obedience, and ultimately following that obedience to the cross (Luke 22:42), the Lord Jesus was *made perfect* by His father. Unlike anyone else in all of history, the Lord was resurrected from death and given *immortality*. He would never die again. And the possibility of sin was no more. He was perfect.

In these words, we see one of the ways in which Scripture uses the idea of perfection. Perfection isn't fine-tuning a process at work until there are no mistakes—at least Scripturally. Perfection, used in this way, isn't simply never sinning. Instead, this definition sees perfection as never sinning, *and* having a nature which is never even inclined to sin. In short, this view of perfection is immortality (cp. Philippians 3:12; Hebrews 2:10; Hebrews 7:19; Hebrews 10:1).

And really, that brings us to the power of our consideration today. As we saw in our last few chapters, God made a promise to Abraham: Abraham would one day receive all of the land of Israel (Genesis 13:14-15). But, in his lifetime, that promise was never fulfilled (Acts 7:5). As it would appear, God simply left the promise unfulfilled.

Nevertheless, again in the book of Hebrews, the apostle referred to this very conundrum—and yet he gave us an answer:

"And all these, though commended through their faith, did not receive what was promised, since God had provided something better for us, that apart from us they should not be made perfect." Hebrews 11:39-40

This was where we ended in our last chapter—but at that time we were left wondering what we truly meant by the words "that apart from us they should not be made perfect." And now, after looking at an earlier passage in his epistle, we can better grasp what the author meant.

God prevented the promises from being fulfilled during Abraham's lifetime, and He did it for a specific reason—He did it because His mind was on the future. It wasn't simply that God wanted Abraham and his descendants to inherit the land for just a lifetime. It wasn't that he wanted Abraham to possess the land and then pass it on to his children.

Instead, God wanted Abraham to possess it *forever* (Genesis 13:15). And there was only one time in which that would take place: when all of God's followers were made *perfect*. In other words, from the very beginning, God intended to bring about the fulfillment of this promise after Abraham and his offspring were given immortality.

And yet, again, there's another conundrum bound up in these words—because, if indeed the things that are commonly taught in the Churches about the immortality of the soul and the afterlife are true, then wouldn't Abraham and his offspring *already* be made perfect?

But, as the writer to the Hebrews said, this perfection was something that *hadn't yet taken place:* "that apart from us they should not be made perfect."

Abraham isn't yet perfect. Abraham isn't yet immortal.

So then, where is he now? What does that mean about life after death? And what does that mean for us?

Chapter 10 - Resurrection

Our last chapter unearthed an idea that might have been a bit unsettling: Abraham, as it would appear, has not yet been made perfect. As we said, he isn't immortal—at least right now.

Thus, what does that mean about life after death? And how does that affect us?

First of all, lest we feel apprehensive, let's just consider again exactly what it was that the writer to the Hebrews had said about not only Abraham, but all of the faithful:

"And all these, though commended through their faith, did not receive what was promised, since God had provided something better for us, that apart from us they should not be made perfect." Hebrews 11:39-40

Though all of these people—Abraham, Sarah, Isaac, Samson, Gideon, etc.—had been commended for their faith, they had not yet been made perfect. It hadn't happened at that point—but here's what's important: it *eventually would.* Thus, by no means was the apostle attempting to say that there was no hope after death. To the contrary, he was teaching that indeed there *was hope*—but, it would appear as though that hope comes at a very different time than many of us may have initially been taught.

Perfection doesn't come as soon as we die. Instead, it comes at a certain point when all of the faithful will be given it *at the same time.* "That apart from us they should not be made perfect."

So, when is it that *all of us together* will be made perfect? Or, put another way, when will all of the faithful be given immortality?

The apostle Paul provides a straightforward answer to our question:

"Behold! I tell you a mystery. We shall not all sleep, but we shall all be changed, in a moment, in the twinkling of an eye, at the last trumpet. For the trumpet will sound, and the dead will be raised imperishable, and we shall be changed." 1 Corinthians 15:51-52

Did you notice that the apostle used similar language to the writer to the Hebrews? He wasn't talking about another group in the distant past—he said: "we shall all be changed." All of those to whom he was writing! This was something that would affect all of the faithful. He was writing about a time when all of the faithful would be changed and given immortality— when they would be made "imperishable."

And did you notice when that was?

Consistent with what we saw in the book of Hebrews, it *wasn't* right after they died. Instead, the apostle stated, "the dead will be raised." These are words about the resurrection!

As it would appear, perfection comes, not after death, but after the resurrection! Again, the same thing is consistently taught throughout all of Scripture (Daniel 12:2; 1 Thessalonians 4:16-17). The resurrection is the time when we are all changed.

And so, Abraham waits in the grave—but not forever. God made a promise, and that promise will undoubtedly be fulfilled. Abraham will be given the land, but it will be given after the resurrection.

And yet, that leads us to another question—if the resurrection is the time when *all* of the faithful will be given life eternal, then why don't we often hear about it? And, when will it take place?

Chapter 11 - The Last Day

As we've journeyed together through the promises to Abraham, we've seen some things that have perhaps surprised us. While we may have initially known about these promises, perhaps we hadn't yet seen that they haven't been fulfilled. At the same time, perhaps we also hadn't ever realized that they were connected to our own hope and that they impacted us.

And perhaps in this chapter, we'll look at the greatest surprise of all: life after death.

In our last chapter, we investigated the idea of the resurrection—and we saw that implicit within the promises to Abraham was the plan of a resurrection. Abraham hasn't received the promises; and yet, it isn't because God simply made a promise and decided not to fulfill it—far be it from Him! Instead, they're unfulfilled specifically because He wants *all* of His followers to receive the promises at the same time!

And—and this is a *big* "and"—the writer to the Hebrews didn't simply say that God wanted all of His followers to receive the promises at the same time, but he, by divine inspiration, used a significant word to describe the fulfillment of those promises. He said that their fulfillment would be when the believers would be made "perfect" (Hebrews 11:40).

In other words, the promises to Abraham will be fulfilled at the resurrection, and it will be at that time that God will make His followers *perfect.* Before we move on, just think a little bit about what that means and the impact that it has on Abraham *today.*

The implications are pretty huge. If Abraham is waiting to be made *perfect,* then what state is he in right now? And if such is the case with Abraham, then what about the rest of those who have died and are waiting for the fulfillment of those promises?

As it would appear, contrary to what is often taught from the pulpits today, if we believe in the promises to Abraham and we understand what the writer to the Hebrews was emphasizing about their fulfillment, then we come to the conclusion that at this present moment, neither Abraham nor any of the other faithful have been made perfect—they have not been given immortality. Unlike typical Christian tradition, they aren't up in heaven, living eternally, or living as some type of immortal spirit being.

Instead, they're waiting to be changed. They're waiting for the Lord Jesus to come and begin the *resurrection*—something which has consistently been the belief of those who have had followed the faith of Abraham. Here are just a couple of examples:

Jesus: "Do not marvel at this, for an hour is coming when all who are in the tombs will hear his voice and come out, those who have done good to the resurrection of life, and those who have done evil to the resurrection of judgment." John 5:28-29

Martha: "Jesus said to her, 'Your brother will rise again.' Martha said to him, 'I know that he will rise again in the resurrection on the last day.' John 11:23-24

The Apostle Paul: "But this I confess to you, that according to the Way, which they call a sect, I worship the God of our fathers, believing everything laid down by the Law and written in the Prophets, 15 having a hope in God, which these men themselves accept, that there will be a resurrection of both the just and the unjust." Acts 24:14-15

The Lord Jesus spoke of a "resurrection to life"—a time when the faithful will be given perfection. Martha, even though her brother Lazarus had died, knew that she would see him again, not in *heaven,* but "in the resurrection on the last day." When defending his hope to the Roman governor Felix, the apostle Paul didn't say that he hoped for eternal life in heaven—his hope was very specific: "that there will be a resurrection of both the just and the unjust."

And, did you notice when that hope would come to fruition? As Martha said: "on the last day." The resurrection, the hope of the faithful, isn't something that they receive at death—but it is something that they receive in the last days, at the return of the Lord Jesus to this earth.

Thus, the promises to Abraham lead us to a conclusion that is perhaps surprising: the hope of Abraham—and even the belief of all of the faithful throughout the centuries, even of Jesus himself, has not been the hope of heaven-going, but instead, has been the hope of a resurrection.

Chapter 12 - The Land

Abraham is dead. King David is dead. All of the faithful of old—they're all dead (Hebrews 11:13). But they will live again.

We noted in our last chapter that the believers' hope isn't what is typically taught in the churches—that of heaven-going after death—but is the hope of a resurrection *at the last day*. It's the hope that at the "time of the end," when Jesus returns to this earth, a resurrection will take place.

It's at the resurrection that these promises will be fulfilled. Finally, after so many centuries and so many millennia, these unbreakable promises will be fully realized.

But what does that mean?

Well, just consider the aspect of the promises that haven't yet come to pass: Abraham and his descendants indeed were already made a great nation (Genesis 12:2); Abraham was blessed (Genesis 12:2); his name was made great (Genesis 12:2); those who blessed him were blessed and those who dishonored him were cursed (Genesis 12:3); all families of the earth were blessed through Abraham, since the Lord Jesus Christ is a direct descendant from him (Genesis 12:3; cp. Acts 3:25-26); but, there is *one* part of the promise that hasn't yet been fulfilled:

"The Lord said to Abram, after Lot had separated from him, 'Lift up your eyes and look from the place where you are, northward and southward and eastward and westward, for all the land that you see I will give to you and to your offspring forever.'" Genesis 13:14-15

Abraham was promised *the land.*

While it's possible to make a case that indeed the land *was* given to Abraham, Isaac, and Jacob's seed (Deuteronomy 1:7-9), and even at this time *is* possessed by the nation of Israel, there are still a few unresolved questions:

- The land promised to Abraham stretched from Egypt to Iran (Genesis 15:18)—a swath of territory which is not even *remotely* controlled by modern Israel.
- And, the land wasn't simply promised to Abraham's seed, but to *Abraham!*

Once again, just to remind ourselves, consider what Stephen said about the fulfillment of this promise— specifically the promise of the land:

"Yet he gave him no inheritance in it, not even a foot's length, but promised to give it to him as a possession and to his offspring after him, though he had no child." Acts 7:5

Abraham *never* received the land! And thus, while all of the promises were essentially fulfilled, it is this aspect of the promises that demands resurrection and which will indeed be fulfilled when faithful Abraham is given new life at the "last day." After so many years, Abraham will be given the land that eluded him all of his life.

And, not only will Abraham be given the land, but it will be given to his seed as well—the words of the promises themselves dictate this: "for all the land that you see I will give you and to your offspring forever."

There's an eternal element here—an eternal element that necessitates *resurrection* and eternal life.

And thus we see all of these ideas beautifully coalescing. The promises have not been fulfilled—because one aspect of them, specifically, the promise of the land, has not yet been completed. Abraham is dead. But one day, when the dead are raised, the promise will be fulfilled and he will be given the land. And not just him, but his "offspring" too.

But who are they? And does that really matter to those of us who aren't actually Jews?

Chapter 13 - The Children

"The children of Abraham" is a term that probably isn't significant to us.

But it should be.

It is a term that is central to what we've explored so far on this topic—over and over Abraham was promised that God would multiply his "offspring," or his descendants (Genesis 13:16; Genesis 15:5). Repeatedly, the promises made to Abraham were extended to his children (Genesis 12:7; Genesis 13:15; Genesis 15:18). The seed of Abraham—the people who descended from him, are *crucial* to our understanding of the promises!

And yet, their identity might be entirely different than what we expected.

As far as bloodlines go, the natural descendants of Abraham, at least the descendants who are referred to in the promises, are the Jews. The promise was given to Abraham, reiterated to Isaac (Genesis 17:19), and then passed on to Jacob (Genesis 28:13)—whose name was eventually changed to "Israel" (Genesis 32:28). Thus, the promise was given to the Jews.

Therefore, with that background, it would seem clear that we would expect the Jewish people to inherit the promises. They would be the ones who would possess the land. They would be the ones through whom the world would be blessed.

And indeed, in a sense, that is true. The land of Israel was given to the Jewish people (Deuteronomy 1:8). The Lord Jesus Christ was a Jew (John 4:9), and it is through him that all nations can be blessed (Acts 3:26).

But at the same time, there is much more to this.

While the promises were made to Abraham and his descendants, the beautiful gift of God is that the term "descendants" doesn't simply refer to Abraham's natural descendants. Just consider what the Lord Jesus Christ says about Abraham's children:

"They answered him, 'Abraham is our father.' Jesus said to them, 'If you were Abraham's children, you would be doing the works Abraham did.'" John 8:39

Notice what the Lord Jesus Christ just did—in speaking to the Jews, he told them that there was more to being Abraham's children than simply bloodlines. It wasn't about who their natural father was. John the Baptist stated the same thing, preaching that God could raise up natural children to Abraham out of stones (Matthew 3:9)! It wasn't genealogy that mattered. Instead, it was an attitude and action. Those who lived like Abraham were invited to be a part of his family. Again, the same thing is affirmed later by the apostle Paul:

"For as many of you as were baptized into Christ have put on Christ...And if you are Christ's, then you

are Abraham's offspring, heirs according to promise."
Galatians 3:27, 29

When we are baptized—when we commit our lives to God and Christ, we are following the faithful devotion of Abraham! And therefore, we are joining his family!

Just think about what this means. Most of us are probably not Jewish. We aren't literal descendants of Abraham. As such, these promises—these promises that contain hope and a promise of resurrection—have nothing to do with us!

But they can—and that's the blessing about these promises. These promises, that were made so long ago, to a man that has no connection to us, can become promises that envelop our lives, and that changes everything.

For our part, we must learn to live in faith like Abraham—and the first step in that, as the apostle Paul stated, is baptism.

And yet, there's a bit more for us to explore there—why baptism? Why is it that this step is so essential, and how is it that it is connected explicitly to the promises to Abraham?

Chapter 14 - The Heir

Why does baptism matter? And why do some churches baptize children, while others baptize adults? And why is baptism connected to the promises made to Abraham?

The promises made to Abraham are overarching promises that speak of blessings, of land, and of a nation. Yet for many of us, they are promises from which we seem to be excluded—because they were promises that were made to a Jew and were passed on to his Jewish descendants. Being Gentiles, many of us have nothing to do with them. Such was the state that the believers in Ephesus found themselves. Before they came to know the Lord Jesus Christ, they were "strangers" from these promises:

"Remember that you were at that time separated from Christ, alienated from the commonwealth of Israel and strangers to the covenants of promise, having no hope and without God in the world." Ephesians 2:12

Consider the implications of this verse—because they are huge. Essentially, in being born Gentiles and not Jews, these Greeks had *nothing*. They were "alienated from the commonwealth of Israel and strangers to the covenants of promise," thus they had nothing to do with the promises, and because of that, they had *no hope!*

And thus, for those of us who are Gentiles, born outside of the seed of Abraham, we are naturally *strangers* to those promises.

But, as we noted in the last chapter, all of this can change through baptism—and what we really want to note now is *why* that change takes place. Consider again the apostle's words about the relationship between baptism and the promises:

"For as many of you as were baptized into Christ have put on Christ…And if you are Christ's, then you are Abraham's offspring, heirs according to promise." Galatians 3:27, 29

By being baptized, we become heirs of the promises made to Abraham—and yet we really want to focus on the *reason* for that connection. The apostle made it plain: when we are baptized into Christ, we are putting Christ on, as though we are putting on a garment! We are coming into Christ! By coming into him, we become *part* of the one who was the true heir, the true seed of Abraham through which the rest of the world will be blessed (Acts 3:26). And by becoming part of him, we commit to trying to *be* like him—we die to sin and live for God, just as Christ literally did through the cross and his resurrection (Romans 6:1-6). Think about what that means—and think about the implications for baptism.

Baptism isn't just getting wet. Baptism is *associating* ourselves with the Lord Jesus Christ. Baptism is a conscious acknowledgment that we want to be *heirs* of the promise and we want to be part of the body of Christ (1 Corinthians 12). And we want to *follow* the Lord Jesus.

Not only, then, is this a decision that should be made by adults who know what it is that they are choosing, but this is a decision that is *essential* for believers! Baptism isn't optional (Mark 16:16). For all of those who want to become heirs of the promises, they must join themselves to Christ—the true heir. We must take hold of this grace and not let it go!

Yet at the same time, this plan also displays God's mercy: the very fact that we, frail humans who constantly fall in our mistakes (Romans 7:15-24), could be joined to the *only perfect man in all of history* and could "put" him "on" as a covering is simply beautiful. When we are baptized, not only are we becoming heirs to the promises, but we are joining ourselves to perfection because we are committing to try to live as he did. Thus, as long as we continue to strive to be like him, we can be seen as part of the Lord Jesus Christ. This is the means by which our sins can be washed away.

Indeed, in baptism we not only see the grace of God in giving us something that we don't deserve, but we see His mercy in covering over what we do deserve. Truly, if that doesn't move us and bring us to our knees in gratitude, then perhaps there isn't much that will.

Part 2

The Good News
of Jesus Christ

Section 3
A Reflection of God

Chapter 15 - Mysteries

Have you ever asked a question and been told that the answer is a *mystery?*

Maybe your question was about God's origins, or maybe it was in search of a deeper understanding of God's nature.

Typically, when we're told that the answer to our question is a *mystery,* by implication, our question has no answer. We could try to probe it further, but it's likely that we will simply think ourselves in circles and just won't be able to find an answer. At least, that's what the term mystery implies.

Nevertheless, there's something beautiful about mysteries when we come to Scripture, because Scriptural mysteries are entirely different than everyday mysteries. Scriptural mysteries are more like *secrets* that God keeps from some people and reveals to others. Here are a few examples—look for what they have in common:

"And the disciples came, and said unto him, Why speakest thou unto them in parables? He answered and said unto them, Because it is given unto you to know the mysteries of the kingdom of heaven, but to them it is not given." Matthew 13:10-11 KJV

"Lest you be wise in your own sight, I do not want you to be unaware of this mystery, brothers: a partial hardening has come upon Israel, until the fullness of the Gentiles has come in." Romans 11:25

"Making known to us the mystery of his will, according to his purpose, which he set forth in Christ." Ephesians 1:9

These three verses all use the word "mystery" or "mysteries," and they all use them in the same way—and in fact, the word is almost *always* used this way throughout all of Scripture. In these verses, "mystery," is a secret that has been revealed to the believers, but is hidden to the rest of the world.

Just consider the Lord's words in Matthew. He had just told the parable of the sower—the parable in which a man takes his seed and scatters it over the ground, with some landing on the path, some landing in stony ground, others landing in thorny ground, and others in good ground. It was the first parable that the Lord ever told. Afterward, his disciples came to him and asked why he spoke in parables. His answer: because to *them* it had been given to know the mysteries of God's kingdom, but to the other listeners it had not been given. In other words, Christ's parable was about the kingdom, and his disciples would understand that (Matthew 13:18-23), and yet for many, this deeper meaning would remain a mystery.

Essentially, the Lord Jesus explained that a *Scriptural mystery* is quite different than our everyday mystery. Unlike the mysteries that we encounter, Scriptural mysteries always have a group of people who *know* the answer—because these mysteries were made by an omniscient God who chose to reveal their answers in His word. Scriptural mysteries are *understood by believers,* but confused by the world.

Thus, as you read through Scripture, just look for this association—over and over, whenever the term "mystery" appears, it is soon be followed by a sentence that *explains* what the mystery is, or that states that the mystery has been revealed to believers (Romans 16:25; 1 Corinthians 2:7; Ephesians 3:3; Revelation 17:7).

But really, this just opens up more questions for us: if this indeed is the case, then *why* is it that God has chosen to use mysteries this way? Why not simply reveal the answer to everyone? And even more, how do we know if a question is a Scriptural mystery, and thus we should continue to search the Bible for an answer, or if it really doesn't have an answer?

Chapter 16 - Purposefully Confusing?

One of my favorite verses is in Proverbs. You may have come across it before in your reading:

"It is the glory of God to conceal things, but the glory of kings is to search things out." Proverbs 25:2

Though this verse may, at first glance, not even seem as though it applies to us, it lays out a beautiful principle: God is a God of mysteries, and it is the job of kings, or even the *privilege* of kings, to search those mysteries out.

As we consider the idea of Scriptural mysteries—the subject of our last chapter, and of a few more to come —this verse is extremely pertinent. Really, it gives us a foundation upon which to base all of our understanding. In coming to Scripture, we must recognize that God is a God of mysteries—*and,* that He expects those mysteries to be understood!

Have you ever sat down, read Scripture, and thought "Wow, that's confusing," or "I really didn't understand what that was about at all"? If you have, and if you've ever felt discouraged because of it, take heart! That's the modus operandi of Scripture. God has hidden mysteries all throughout this book.

Nevertheless, we can't simply stop at the point of confusion. Remember the principle—God is a God of mysteries, but it is the privilege of kings to search things out! Therefore, when we feel confused or when we feel as though Scripture has gone over our heads, we need to ask questions, and we need to search for answers. We need to pray. We need to keep reading! Most of all, we cannot merely stop at the point of confusion.

Our God wants us to search.

And, if we search, He's promised something astonishing: He will give us the answers. Remember the words of the Lord Jesus?

"Ask, and it will be given to you; seek, and you will find; knock, and it will be opened to you. For everyone who asks receives, and the one who seeks finds, and to the one who knocks it will be opened." Matthew 7:7-8

God has hidden mysteries in His Word—and He *wants* people to search for them! He wants people to *long* to know what Scripture means. And, for those who do so—for those who "ask," they will receive. Those who seek will find. This is the way in which God operates, and so we see this principle appear over and over (Proverbs 2:1-5; Proverbs 8:17; James 1:5).

Now, this isn't to say that if we have a question, we pray about it, and then skim through the Bible for a few minutes that we will find the answer. Nor is it to say that if we spend hours pouring through the Word, then we will finally come to the correct conclusion. But it's to say that if we keep reading and keep praying, *eventually* (that's the key word!), the mysteries that have been hidden in Scripture will be revealed to us.

So, our God is a God of mysteries. And He will eventually reveal those mysteries to those who search. But why? Why conceal the mysteries in the first place? Why not reveal them to *everyone?*

Chapter 17 - Searching

Do you have a favorite parable?

Maybe you grew up hearing about the Good Samaritan—the one who stopped and helped the man who had been left on the side of the road. Or, perhaps you were always intrigued by the parable of the vineyard, in which the tenants of the vineyard refused to give the harvest to its owner. Or, maybe you like fishing—and so the parable of the net always resonated with you.

For me, I've always liked the parable of the sower. It's the first parable that the Lord Jesus told, and unlike many of the others, the interpretation follows almost directly after. In the story, a sower walks all around the land, casting seed on the ground. Some of the seed lands on the walking path, where it is crushed by those who walk by. Some of the seed falls on stony ground, and so they grew up quickly, but also withered quickly—because they were not able to make solid roots. Another group of seeds fell in thorny ground, and they too perished, because the thorns choked them. Finally, the last group of seeds fell on good ground, and they grew up to be healthy and strong.

In his interpretation of this parable, the Lord Jesus told his disciples that these four types of ground represented four types of people and their responses to the gospel. The whole parable wasn't just a fable—a story with a nice moral at the end—but it was a symbolic story. Each character and each piece of the story represented something else. The seed represented the word of God (Luke 8:11). The different types of ground represented different kinds of people (Luke 8:12-15).

Nevertheless, just consider that this explanation was *only given* to his disciples. The Lord Jesus told the story, and *then* sometime afterward, his disciples came to him and asked him what it all meant. It was then that he gave them the interpretation (Matthew 13:18-23).

Just consider for a while what that meant.

The disciples came to the Lord Jesus Christ because they heard his story and they did not understand. They were not sure what all of the symbols represented and how they all came together. Nevertheless, they later understood, because the Lord explained it to them—and to them only!

But, what about all of those who simply heard the story?

For many of them, they would have heard the story, perhaps thought it was entertaining or interesting, and then returned home and forgotten what it was all about. Really, it was only those who *came to the Lord Jesus Christ and asked* who were given an explanation! All of those who didn't take the time to *search out* the meaning would have simply missed the depth and the purpose of Christ's words.

Thus, it really leads us to ask a question: why, then, did the Lord Jesus Christ teach in parables? And really, that leads us to the same question that we asked in the last chapter—why would God purposefully make His word difficult to understand?

Well, just after this parable, the disciples asked the Lord the same thing:

"And the disciples came, and said unto him, Why speakest thou unto them in parables? He answered and said unto them, Because it is given unto you to know the mysteries of the kingdom of heaven, but to them it is not given. For whosoever hath, to him shall be given, and he shall have more abundance: but whosoever hath not, from him shall be taken away even that he hath." Matthew 13:10-12

Why did the Lord speak in parables? Why did he make his teaching difficult to understand? The Lord's answer made it clear: there were two groups of people—those who, like the disciples, would eventually understand, and those who, like everyone else who heard the parable, would just return home and never think about it.

The former group, indeed, was the one who was blessed with knowledge. In fact, they were blessed, not just with the interpretation of the parable, but with the *mysteries of the kingdom.*

And why were they blessed with that knowledge?

Undoubtedly it was because of the grace of God—God revealed it to them. But on their end, it was revealed to them because they asked. Unlike the latter group, which merely went home, they *wanted to know* about the "mysteries of the kingdom," and so they earnestly desired that the Lord would reveal them.

Unlike what might seem intuitive, God makes His teaching difficult to understand—and so did the Lord Jesus Christ. Why? Because they are looking for those who search. They are looking for those who come across the mysteries of the kingdom, and who don't just simply turn away from them because they are "mysteries," but who turn through the pages of Scripture, who pray for understanding, and who pour themselves out in a desire to honestly know the God of Scripture, and His son the Lord Jesus Christ.

Who will we be?

Chapter 18 - God's Revelation

At the end of the book of Deuteronomy, Moses made a very striking statement:

"The secret things belong to the LORD our God, but the things that are revealed belong to us and to our children forever, that we may do all the words of this law." Deuteronomy 29:29

In this statement, there is a clear division: there are things that can be understood and things that cannot. Consider, then, how that fits with what we have already seen.

We have seen that God speaks in *mysteries*, and He does this in order to make them purposefully difficult! Nevertheless, God is not a God of confusion (1 Corinthians 14:33), instead, He is a God of peace. While His words can be complicated and hard to understand, there *are* answers—thus, He has purposefully made it challenging in order to sift through those who are willing to search and those who are not.

Rather than telling us to simply be content with what we know, this verse in Deuteronomy is a charge—it is a charge to us, and a charge to anyone who will listen. God has revealed Himself in Scripture. Everything there is part of "the things that are revealed," which are referred to in Deuteronomy. There are the things that "belong to us." We need to cherish them, we need to treasure them, we need to *read* them.

Have you ever found yourself wondering about an important Scriptural topic and feeling like you just don't understand it?

What has been your reaction?

Have you merely been content not to know the answer? Or have you yearned to know more—yearned to know what Scripture *really* says?

The truths contained in the Bible are the things which God has revealed. He has given them to us in order to reveal His mysteries!

And so, when it comes to the question of God's nature—when we start to look at the Trinity and try to understand *who* God really is—we must *pour* through Scripture, sifting through its teaching, realizing that it's going to be difficult to understand. And yet, at the same time, we must also recognize that there *is* an answer.

In other words, if we truly believe that God's nature and His character are revealed in Scripture, then we *cannot* simply say that they are a mystery. Scriptural mysteries, as we have seen in a previous chapter, are things that are *hidden to the world,* but *revealed to the believers.*

Believing that the nature of God is a mystery can become a scary excuse. When really, what God ultimately desires is for us to *know Him,* not to shy away from who He is, claiming that it is a "mystery":

"And this is eternal life, that they know you the only true God, and Jesus Christ whom you have sent." John 17:3

Indeed, isn't that one of the primary goals of all of Scripture—to bring us nearer to our God and to allow us to really *know* Him?

Therefore, in the next few chapters, we'll explore how God has truly revealed Himself throughout His Word.

Chapter 19 - The Angels

What do you think about when you consider the angels?

Do you think about little cherub-like beings that fly around somehow and manipulate the world? Or maybe you think about human-like figures with majestic wings and shimmering halos. Or, perhaps, you think about beings that look just like men and women.

Angels are perhaps one of the more misunderstood characters in Scripture. The actual picture that Scripture paints of angels is one of eternal beings who follow God's will, who wield His authority, and who represent Him in everything that they do. Oftentimes they are simply described as looking like humans, although they have also appeared in a fiery pillar, a cloud, and, really, whatever else they may need to look like in order to accomplish God's will.

This is their primary purpose: the fulfillment of God's will.

Just consider some of the following pictures of angels:

When God determined that it was time to destroy Sodom and Gomorrah, He sent two angels to the city to accomplish that destruction and to rescue Lot, one of God's servants who still lived there (Genesis 19:1). When Jacob, the patriarch of Israel, arrived in Egypt, he described the way in which God had been with him: there had been an angel leading him all along (Genesis 48:16). When Moses stood before the burning bush, the words of God were conveyed to him by an angel (Exodus 3:2). And, when the law of Moses was given to the people, it was given to them by the angels (Galatians 3:19).

The angels are God's messengers and God's servants. They do His will and they act on His behalf. Whatever it is that God wants done, the angels bring it to pass.

This work is summarized beautifully in a verse in the psalms and a verse in Hebrews:

"Bless the LORD, O you his angels, you mighty ones who do his word, obeying the voice of his word." Psalm 103:20

"Are they not all ministering spirits sent out to serve for the sake of those who are to inherit salvation?" Hebrews 1:14

The angels do God's word and minister to those who will be the heirs of salvation.

Such is their task and such is their desire.

And yet, there is one other major charge that the angels are given, and this charge makes a crucial difference in the way that we understand the God of the Bible. This charge can be seen in each of the pictures of angels that were mentioned above, and it unifies them all beautifully.

In our next chapter, as we attempt to better understand God and to see the way in which He reveals Himself through Scripture, we will consider this vital charge that has been given to the angels.

Chapter 20 - Bearing God's Name

As God's messengers and God's representatives, the angels have been given the precious charge of bearing God's name. Whatever they do and wherever they go, they represent the One who has commanded and sent them.

In the last chapter, we noted numerous instances in which the angels acted on God's behalf: when God destroyed Sodom and Gomorrah, throughout the entirety of the patriarch Jacob's life, when Moses was at the burning bush, and when the law was given to the children of Israel. In each of these instances, the angels were commanded by God to act, and they acted as His representatives.

Therefore, representing Him, the angels in all four of these accounts were *called by God's name.*

Just consider the story of Sodom and Gomorrah's destruction.

In Genesis 18, Abraham was sitting at the door of his tent when he was approached by three men—one of whom is called "the LORD," or the personal name of God, typically considered to be "Yahweh." Yahweh and the two others proceed to share a meal with Abraham, tell him that he and Sarah would have a son in the next year, and then turn their attention to Sodom and Gomorrah. Yahweh then decides to tell Abraham what He is about to do, and in this disclosure, there is an astonishing statement—a statement that hints at the fact that these three men are actually angels:

"Then the LORD said, 'Because the outcry against Sodom and Gomorrah is great and their sin is very grave, I will go down to see whether they have done altogether according to the outcry that has come to me. And if not, I will know.'" Genesis 18:20-21

Yahweh stated that He would go down and *see if the evil of Sodom and Gomorrah was as great as He had heard!* Consider what that indicates about the one called "the LORD" here—he was not omniscient! Though he was called by God's name, he did not actually know everything, and instead, had to *go down to Sodom* to see if it was actually as wicked as he had heard.

This is perhaps the first indication that "the LORD" who visited Abraham was actually an angel bearing God's name.

But, note what happens:

"So the men turned from there and went toward Sodom, but Abraham still stood before the LORD." Genesis 18:22

Two of the men went to Sodom and Gomorrah, just as "the LORD" had said *he* would do. And, one of the men stays with Abraham, and he is explicitly called by God's name. Thus, two angels do what Yahweh said *He* would do, indicating that they too were bearing God's name, and one man, or angel, continues to stay with Abraham.

The idea that all three of these men were angels is then reinforced in the next chapter, when we are told about the arrival of the two at Sodom:

"The two angels came to Sodom in the evening, and Lot was sitting in the gate of Sodom." Genesis 19:1

Thus their identity is revealed. These two, who were called both "men" and "the LORD" in the previous chapter, are actually angels. They were angels who looked like men, and who, as God's representatives, could be called by His name.

Adding to that, if these two "men" were angels, then what about the one who stayed with Abraham and was called "the LORD"? Wouldn't he also be an angel, considering that he arrived at Abraham's tent with the other two and was described in the same terms? Indeed, but the New Testament leaves us in no doubt, explaining that no man has ever seen Yahweh Himself:

"No one has ever seen God; if we love one another, God abides in us and his love is perfected in us." 1 John 4:12

No one has ever seen God. Therefore, when God appeared to Abraham just before the destruction of Sodom and Gomorrah, it was not God Himself.

Indeed, it was the angels, bearing God's name and acting on His behalf.

In the next chapter, we will see this phenomenon of angels representing God and bearing His name, in those three other instances mentioned above.

Chapter 21 - Appearing to the Patriarchs

"No one has ever seen God."

The apostle John's statement is unequivocal—and he wrote the same phrase twice (John 1:18; 1 John 4:12). No one has *ever* seen God. Jacob, despite being the great patriarch of Israel, never saw him; Moses, the giver of the law, and the "man of God" (Deuteronomy 33:1), never saw him; nor did the children of Israel, though they were God's chosen people. John's statement leaves no room for doubt.

And yet, Scripture does, with this unambiguous statement, create a bit of a paradox—just consider what is recorded of Jacob, Moses, and the elders of Israel:

1 - Jacob: "And he dreamed, and behold, there was a ladder set up on the earth, and the top of it reached to heaven. And behold, the angels of God were ascending and descending on it! And behold, the LORD stood above it and said, 'I am the LORD, the God of Abraham your father and the God of Isaac.'" Genesis 28:12-13

2 - Moses: "Go and gather the elders of Israel together and say to them, 'The LORD, the God of your fathers, the God of Abraham, of Isaac, and of Jacob, has appeared to me.'" Exodus 3:16

3 - The elders of Israel: "Then Moses and Aaron, Nadab, and Abihu, and seventy of the elders of Israel

went up, and they saw the God of Israel." Exodus 24:9-10

While John's statement is quite clear, at the same time, so is the testimony of the Old Testament. Jacob, Moses, and the elders of Israel all *saw God*. The verses appear to present a contradiction, and yet Scripture, being inspired wholly by God, cannot truly have contradictions.

So how can all of these verses work together in harmony?

As is so often the case, Scripture itself provides the answer—and just as we noted in the last chapter about Abraham and the angels, the answer is hidden in the way in which angels represent Yahweh.

1 - Jacob: After Jacob awoke from his dream, the dream in which he saw Yahweh at the top of the ladder, he chose to name the place where had slept "Bethel," which translates to "house of God." Just a few chapters later (although many years later chronologically), an angel appeared to Jacob, and take special note of what this angel said:

"Then the angel of God said to me in the dream, 'Jacob,' and I said, 'Here I am.' And he said...'I am the God of Bethel, where you anointed a pillar and made a vow to me.'" Genesis 31:11-13

This time, Scripture reveals the identity of the one who was "God" in Bethel—it was an angel!

Essentially, Jacob did not literally see God, but he saw an angel representing God! Again, the same thing can be seen with Moses.

2 - Moses: When Moses stood before the burning bush, he was commanded to go before the elders of Israel and declare to them that Yahweh had *appeared* to him. And yet, according to the narrative, note carefully who had *appeared:*

"And the angel of the LORD appeared to him in a flame of fire out of the midst of a bush." Exodus 3:2

Though Moses was told to tell the people that Yahweh had appeared to him, it had literally been an angel—who was bearing God's name and acting as His representative—that had appeared to him.

3 - The elders of Israel: Finally, when the elders of Israel went up to Mount Sinai and saw God, they were in the process of receiving the law. Thus, they met with God and obtained the law from Him.

Nevertheless, note what the New Testament writers state about how the law was given:

"You who received the law as delivered by angels and did not keep it." Acts 7:53

"The law...was put in place through angels." Galatians 3:19

The law was delivered to the people and put into place by the angels! Thus, when the elders of Israel met with God to receive the law, it would seem most probable that they met with an angel who was representing God.

Scripture never contradicts itself. Though no man has ever seen God, the patriarchs, along with many of the faithful of old have indeed seen Him—because they have met with Him through His representatives, namely, the angels.

Yet, there is an even greater representative than the angels, and it is to that most glorious representative that we turn our attention in the next chapter.

Chapter 22 - The Example of the Master

As the Lord Jesus debated with the Jews, he made an unequivocal and categorical statement about his relationship to his Father:

"I and the Father are one." John 10:30

Taken at face value, this statement would seem to straightforwardly and unabashedly teach that the Lord Jesus and His Father were one being, and of one substance—being, as it is so often taught, "co-equal" and "coeternal."

And yet, at the same time, there are a few problems with that understanding of the Lord's statement.

First, while Christ clearly declared his oneness with his Father, he also made a number of statements that just don't fit with this idea of him being "co-equal" with his Father. Just consider what he said, again to the Jews, when he sought to explain to them why he healed a man on the Sabbath:

"So Jesus said to them, 'Truly, truly, I say to you, the Son can do nothing of his own accord, but only what he sees the Father doing. For whatever the Father does, that the Son does likewise.'" John 5:19

Just as God works on the Sabbath (v. 17), the Lord had done the same thing. There was nothing that he did that he did not learn from his Father—his Father taught him everything that he knows. That certainly does not sound like a co-equal relationship. Yet again, just a few verses later, the Lord said the same thing:

"I can do nothing on my own. As I hear, I judge, and my judgment is just, because I seek not my own will but the will of him who sent me." John 5:30

These verses present a problem when we attempt to understand the Lord's relationship within the framework of the Trinity. They simply cannot explain a relationship that is considered co-equal—if one member of the relationship can only do things that the other has taught him, then there must be some sort of inequality! However, perhaps what is most astonishing about this is that in fact, the Lord Jesus made statements like this all throughout the gospel of John—demonstrating his reliance upon his Father and the fact that it was *God's power*, not his own, that allowed him to do anything at all:

"So Jesus answered them, 'My teaching is not mine, but his who sent me.'" John 7:16

"In your Law it is written that the testimony of two people is true. I am the one who bears witness about myself, and the Father who sent me bears witness about me." John 8:17-18

"Jesus answered, 'If I glorify myself, my glory is nothing. It is my Father who glorifies me, of whom you say, 'He is our God.'" John 8:54

"Do you not believe that I am in the Father and the Father is in me? The words that I say to you I do not speak on my own authority, but the Father who dwells in me does his works." John 14:10

"Whoever does not love me does not keep my words. And the word that you hear is not mine but the Father's who sent me." John 14:24

Perhaps the culminating reference in all of this, however, is found just a few verses later. Jesus himself *clearly* explained his relationship to his Father:

"You heard me say to you, 'I am going away, and I will come to you.' If you loved me, you would have rejoiced, because I am going to the Father, for the Father is greater than I." John 14:28

God is greater than Christ. While Christ is mighty, while he has been given "all authority in heaven and on earth" (Matthew 28:18), and while there is no name under heaven by which men can be saved (Acts 4:12), the Lord Jesus is subject to his Father—and that, by the sheer volume of statements above, seems to be a fact that the Lord Jesus wants us to understand.

Therefore, what did the Lord Jesus truly mean when he stated that he was "one" with God? And how can that statement fit with the rest of the passages in this chapter?

Chapter 23 - That They May Be One

In the last chapter, we posited that Christ made very clear statements regarding his status and his Father's status. While he was given all power in heaven and in earth, the Lord Jesus still made it plain that his Father was greater than he.

And thus, with that in mind, what was it that the Lord Jesus meant when he said that he and the Father are one? How could they be one if they are not co-equal?

In a beautiful way, the Lord Jesus himself explained this relationship—because later in the very same gospel where he spoke about his oneness with God, he used the same term to describe the relationship that he wanted the disciples to have:

"I do not ask for these only, but also for those who will believe in me through their word, that they may all be one, just as you, Father, are in me, and I in you, that they also may be in us, so that the world may believe that you have sent me." John 17:20-21

On the last night of Christ's life, he prayed for his disciples, and for all of those who would believe on him through their preaching. And what did the Lord want for them?

"That they may all be one."

And yet, the Master did not leave us without an explanation. It was not just that he wanted his disciples to be one, but that he wanted them to be one "just as you, Father, are in me, and I in you."

The Lord wanted the very oneness that he had claimed with God in John 10:30 to be a oneness that his disciples experienced—both amongst themselves, and also with the Father and the Son!

Even more, if it wasn't clear enough that Christ wanted his disciples to be one with each other and one with him and his Father, he reiterated the idea in the very next verse:

"The glory that you have given me I have given to them, that they may be one even as we are one." John 17:22

This statement is very straightforward: they were to be one *just as* Christ was one with his Father.

How elucidating!

Though there is a temptation to interpret Christ's oneness with his Father to mean that they were of one substance—being co-equal and co-eternal as taught by the Trinity—when we ask questions and allow the Lord Jesus himself to explain the term, the meaning is quite plain. The Lord was not saying that he and the Father were one substance. Otherwise, the disciples would somehow have to attempt to become one substance!

Instead, they were one in mind. And the Lord wanted his followers to be of one mind—both with each other, and with him and the Father.

In other words, when Christ said that he was one with the Father, he was explaining that he was a perfect representative, in a similar, but much greater way, to the way in which the angels represented God in the Old Testament.

And, perhaps what is even more exciting about this conclusion is the fact that even in John 10, just after his statement that he is one with the Father, the Lord Jesus goes on, even there, to explain that it was this oneness of mind and this representative role that he sought to convey to his listeners.

And such is what we will unearth in the next chapter.

Chapter 24 - I Am the Son of God

We've spent some time now looking at this concept of the Lord Jesus being "one" with his Father. By looking at the overall teaching of Scripture, we've realized that indeed, the idea that Christ is co-equal with God is not what the Lord himself taught, and we've also noted that this oneness of which the Lord spoke seemed to be a oneness of mind.

But we haven't yet studied the actual place in which Christ made that claim.

So, let's take a look. Read through these words carefully—and consider the reaction that the Jews have to Christ's words:

"'I and the Father are one.' The Jews picked up stones again to stone him. Jesus answered them, 'I have shown you many good works from the Father; for which of them are you going to stone me?' The Jews answered him, 'It is not for a good work that we are going to stone you but for blasphemy, because you, being a man, make yourself God.'" John 10:30-33

After the Lord made his statement, the Jews were furious. In their mind, there was no question what he was saying: though he were a man, he had just stated that he was God.

In other words, the Jews heard these words and took them in the same way that the Trinitarians do today.

Now, if this were the correct understanding, how would we have expected the Lord Jesus to react? Likely, he would have said something in the affirmative—confirming to them that they had understood him correctly, and then expounding upon the way in which he was indeed God.

But his reaction takes us by surprise:

"Jesus answered them, 'Is it not written in your Law, 'I said, you are gods'?'" John 10:34

Notice that the Lord did not affirm their statement—nor did he deny it. Instead, he latched on to their charge—and explained how it was wrong. They claimed that he had called himself God. Well, he was about to show them that in fact, *their very own rulers* had been called "gods."

Thus, the Lord quoted Psalm 82:6 to them: a psalm that was built upon this very idea of representation.

In that psalm, the rulers of the people were called *gods*—not because they were literally God, or because they were some type of lesser god, but because they represented God. They were to teach the people God's ways. They were to be of one mind with Him and encourage His principles amongst the people.

Even the elders of Israel had been called gods. And so the Jews were going to take offense at him making himself God?

But, in fact—and here is the time that he tells them that their charge was wrong in the first place—that isn't actually what he said in the first place. Read carefully:

"If he called them gods to whom the word of God came—and Scripture cannot be broken—do you say of him whom the Father consecrated and sent into the world, 'You are blaspheming,' because I said, 'I am the Son of God'?" John 10:35-36

If the rulers could have been called gods, then really, there was no issue with the Lord being called "God." Indeed, we saw the same of the angels in the Old Testament.

But, even more than that, the Lord had a greater point to prove. It wasn't just that he could be called God, but in fact *that wasn't what he had said!*

"Because I said, 'I am the Son of God.'"

That was what he meant when he said that he was "one" with God.

The Lord himself explained his words. A son is not the same as his father. But, generally, a son *does* think in the same way as his father.

And so it was with the Lord Jesus. As he said, "The word that you hear is not mine, but the Father's who sent me." John 14:24

Christ didn't just *think* like his Father—but everything he said were God's words. As the son of God, His relationship with the Almighty was unparalleled (John 5:19). God taught him morning by morning (Isaiah 50:4). And he was given the Holy Spirit without measure (John 3:34).

Thus, the Lord was a perfect representative of God. Rather than teaching the Trinity, Scripture teaches that Christ represents his Father—always living by His principles, and always seeking His goals.

And yet, why does this distinction matter? Why does the belief in the Trinity, versus belief in Christ as a representative make a difference?

Chapter 25 - Beliefs Impact Actions

But does it really matter? Is it actually significant that many Christians hold to the idea of the Trinity, versus the doctrine that appears to be taught in Scripture: that of God manifesting Himself in angels and people who represent Him?

Essentially, whenever we are confronted with any kind of discrepancy—be it in a disagreement with a friend or a coworker, be it in some of our own actions, or be it in some of the beliefs that we hold—we must ask ourselves if the discrepancy is significant enough to warrant our consideration. At times, the disagreement may seem so minimal that we might just ignore it, and other times, the controversy requires deeper attention and prayer.

It is my fervent belief that this subject is an example of the latter—and a very serious example at that.

But why? Why is it that a simple belief could be so important?

Because, after all, these are questions about God— and not just questions about His nature, but questions about who He really is. These are questions that impact how we understand the way in which He works in the world. If we desire to know Him, then it behooves us to understand how He reveals Himself. If, as we suggest, He reveals Himself through God manifestation, the implications for us and our lives are huge.

This isn't just an academic question regarding whether or not God is one or three. This is a question that reaches to the very heart of our faith—a question that extends itself, reaching past the nature of God and Christ, and touching the very hope that we take from Scripture. Ultimately, God manifestation is a doctrine that leads us to the end result of what God plans for His followers. It gives a tangible example and provides a framework for hope.

Even more than that, God manifestation impacts our understanding of the cross and what took place there—which in turn, impacts our understanding of the character of God. Depending on our views of this question: "is God a Trinity or does He reveal Himself through God manifestation?" we have a different understanding of what took place on Calvary, and a different understanding of the mercy and love of God.

This is a doctrine with *massive* implications.

Therefore, when we ask ourselves "does this really matter?" the answer must be "yes!"

Because doctrines don't operate in a vacuum. One doctrine impacts another, and eventually, they impact the way in which we act. Beliefs impact actions. Just note the testimony of Hebrews 11, the chapter which is all about faith and its importance:

"By faith Abel offered to God a more acceptable sacrifice than Cain, through which he was commended as righteous, God commending him by accepting his gifts. And through his faith, though he died, he still speaks." Hebrews 11:4

Did you notice *why* Abel offered to God a more excellent sacrifice? What was his motivation?

It was his *faith*. It was his beliefs in what God wanted and who God was. These beliefs *dictated* his actions. Again, consider another of the apostle's examples:

"By faith Noah, being warned by God concerning events as yet unseen, in reverent fear constructed an ark for the saving of his household. By this he condemned the world and became an heir of the righteousness that comes by faith." Hebrews 11:7

What was the motivation for Noah's actions? Again, it was *faith!* His beliefs led to *action*. And so the list goes on. The writer to the Hebrews states that Abraham's faith caused him to be obedient, Isaac's faith caused him to proclaim a blessing on Jacob and Esau, Joseph's faith compelled him to ask for his bones to be brought from Egypt to the promised land.

Over and over, faith—or an understanding of God's character, His promises, and His plan—led to action.

Therefore, this is a doctrine that cannot just be dismissed. The question of the Trinity or God manifestation is a discrepancy that cannot be ignored.

And so in the next chapter, we will consider the far-reaching implications of this doctrine on other doctrines, and ultimately, on our actions.

Chapter 26 - Seeing Christ's Humanity

Belief and doctrines have far-reaching implications. And thus, whether or not the Lord Jesus was part of a Trinity or instead a perfect representative of his Father is not merely a question to be dismissed. It is a question which impacts our understanding of numerous Biblical concepts, and, as emphasized in the last chapter, not only impacts how we think, but how we act.

So, let's just consider an example of how an understanding of the Trinity can color other parts of our understanding:

Perhaps one of the most fundamental beliefs in Christianity is a belief in Christ's death on the cross and his resurrection. And yet, have you ever considered the way in which this belief is thrown into confusion with the doctrine of the Trinity?

A belief in the Trinity is a belief that Jesus, God, and the Holy Spirit are co-equal and co-eternal—thus, by definition, Jesus was never born (since he could not have had a beginning), and he could not possibly have died. He was and always has been *immortal*.

How can this fit? Was Christ's death on the cross simply an act? Or, since, according to the teaching of the Trinity, he was both God and man, did only the "man" portion of him die? Yet, if that is the case, then did he really die?

The Trinity simply throws confusion on one of the most basic and essential teachings of Christianity!

And yet, God manifestation presents the issue in brilliant clarity: God is immortal (1 Timothy 1:17). Jesus was not—thus, as a *man,* he was born and he died. Though he was God's son, he shared our nature. He did not have inherent immortality. After his death, he was resurrected from the grave and *given immortality,* just as those who follow his steps expect to be given immortality (Romans 2:7).

Again, consider another example:

Throughout his life, the Lord Jesus was clearly tempted by sin. This is part of what makes him such an effective and empathetic high priest, as argued in the book of Hebrews:

"For we do not have a high priest who is unable to sympathize with our weaknesses, but one who in every respect has been tempted as we are, yet without sin." Hebrews 4:15

He was tempted in every way that we are—but he never sinned. Such is one of the things that simply makes him amazing. Whereas so many of us fall to temptation, he was tempted, but, through the power of the Spirit, he never gave in to the temptations.

But, once again, the doctrine of the Trinity turns the temptations of Christ into confusion—because the apostle James is very clear about God's relationship to temptation:

"Let no one say when he is tempted, 'I am being tempted by God,' for God cannot be tempted with evil, and he himself tempts no one." James 1:13

God cannot be tempted with evil. There is no loophole in that verse, and there is no wiggle-room. It is simple and straightforward: God cannot be tempted.

So what should be done with Christ's temptations?

Well, from a Trinitarian point of view, with a God and a Christ who cannot be tempted, all of Jesus's temptations turn into a very strange event. Clearly, they happened, as Scripture relates, but they couldn't possibly have happened—because God cannot be tempted with evil. The Trinity turns Christ's temptations into an episode of contradictions.

But, with God manifestation, Christ's temptations are plain. He was a man who represented his Father. As a man, he could be tempted by sin. But, choosing to continue to perfectly represent God, he stood against those temptations—and thus, understood what it meant to truly be tempted, and what it meant to truly resist temptations.

Doctrines do not operate within a vacuum. Our beliefs are interconnected—with one hinging on the other, and when one belief is wrong, it begins to taint other beliefs until confusion results.

And yet, it isn't just that wrong doctrines create confusion—they also lead to wrong actions. As noted previously, doctrines impact actions.

And that, we will demonstrate, in the next chapter.

Chapter 27 - Supersessionism

Have you ever heard the term *supersessionism?*

Or perhaps, have you ever been introduced to *replacement theology?*

The two ideas are essentially synonyms for one another—supersessionism and replacement theology are both names for the Christian teaching that asserts that the Jews were originally God's chosen people, but because they rejected Christ, they were *replaced* by the Church. As a result of this replacement, the Jews lost all of their divine privileges and instead were cursed—cursed to suffer and cursed to wander the earth. Replacement theology is a belief that led to Christian hatred of the Jews. Consider some of the things that Christian leaders wrote and said about the Jewish people:

- Tertullian, a second-century church leader who actually coined the term "Trinity," taught: "Though Israel may wash all its members every day, it is never clean. Its hands, at least, are always stained, forever red with the blood of the prophets and of our Lord himself."[1]

- Gregory of Nyssa, a church leader from the fourth century, took this teaching to the next level, referring to Jews as: "Slayers of the Lord, murderers of the prophets, enemies of God, haters

---

[1] *De Oratione,* 14.1.

of God, adversaries of grace, enemies of their fathers' faith, advocates of the devil, brood of vipers, slanderers, scoffers, men of darkened minds, leaven of the Pharisees, congregation of demons, sinners, wicked men, stoners, and haters of goodness."[2]

- John Chrysostom, a fourth-century Christian leader, preached frightening words: "Just so the Jewish people were driven by their drunkenness and plumpness to the ultimate evil; they kicked about, they failed to accept the yoke of Christ, nor did they pull the plow of his teaching...Although such beasts are unfit for work, they are fit for killing. And this is what happened to the Jews: while they were making themselves unfit for work, they grew fit for slaughter."[3]

- Martin Luther, one of the founders of the Protestant movement, wrote: "What shall we Christians do with this rejected and condemned people, the Jews? Since they live among us, we dare not tolerate their conduct, now that we are aware of their lying and reviling and blaspheming. If we do, we become sharers in their lies, cursing and blasphemy...First to set fire to their synagogues or schools and to bury and cover with dirt whatever will not burn, so that no man will ever again see a stone or cinder of them. This is to

---

[2] Quoted from Fr. Edward Flannery, *The Anguish of the Jews: Twenty-three Centuries of Antisemitism* (Mahwah: Paulist Press, 2004), 50.

[3] *Adversus Judaeos*, Homily 1:2:5-6.

be done in honor of our Lord and of Christendom...Second, I advise that their houses also be razed and destroyed."[4]

For centuries in Christian Europe, from the Crusades (of whom Jews were some of the first victims) to the Spanish Inquisition (whose primary targets were Jews called *conversos*), and even in some ways to the Holocaust, this Christian anti-Judaism, created out of replacement theology, has had terrible results.

And yet, is replacement theology Biblical? And, is this hatred of the Jews Biblical?

Certainly not—the apostle Paul himself provides a straightforward answer:

"I ask, then, has God rejected his people? By no means! For I myself am an Israelite, a descendant of Abraham, a member of the tribe of Benjamin." Romans 11:1

By no means has God rejected the Jews! Indeed, they rejected their Messiah—but as Paul goes on to show, God has never ceased working with them (Romans 11:2-6), and at Christ's second coming, they will receive him and recognize him (Romans 11:25-26).

So from whence came this replacement theology? And where did this dreadful hatred originate?

---

[4] "The Jews and Their Lies," *Jewish Virtual Library*, accessed March 21st, 2014, http://www.jewishvirtuallibrary.org/jsource/anti-semitism/Luther_on_Jews.html.

Replacement theology exists because of another doctrine: the doctrine of the Trinity. Because, if Jesus were God, then it wasn't just that the Jews rejected their Messiah and crucified him, but they *crucified God*. What crime could *ever* be worse? And, how could a people possibly be forgiven for *killing God?* In fact, Trinitarian Christianity even developed a term for the Jewish killing of God: it was termed the crime of deicide.

Whereas the apostle Paul, not believing in a Trinity, could write that the Jews were *not replaced* and not cast off, Tertullian, in his Trinitarian mindset, could see no way in which the Jews could ever have a relationship with God.

And thus began Christian hatred of the Jews.

Is that to say that every Christian who believes in the Trinity will hate the Jews? Certainly not. But, for those Trinitarians who think through their beliefs and who realize that indeed, a belief in the Trinity leads to charging the Jews with deicide, it is difficult to escape some form of anti-Judaism. And, there isn't much distance between anti-Judaism and hatred of the Jews.

Indeed, doctrines impact actions. And tragically, for many Jews, the un-Biblical doctrine of the Trinity has indirectly caused much tragedy.

So let us further examine our beliefs—to ensure that they are in line with Scripture, and that they lead to Scriptural actions that will please the Father and His son.

Section 4
The Beginning of the New Creation

Chapter 28 - The Son of Man

Having considered some of the implications of the doctrine of the Trinity, now consider some of the implications of God manifestation.

A man and a woman nestled close together as they clutched their precious bundle in their arms. Their surroundings weren't exactly what they had expected, but they worked well enough. It was a night which they would never forget—that night, while being the night in which a son was brought into the world, was the night in which the savior of all humanity had come into existence. The Lord Jesus Christ had been born.

For ages, the coming of a divine savior was something which had been expected by the faithful Jews. Prophecy after prophecy pointed towards a Messiah who would be the son of God. In one of the psalms, King David wrote of this Messiah and his kingdom:

"'As for me, I have set my King on Zion, my holy hill.' I will tell of the decree: The Lord said to me, 'You are my Son; today I have begotten you.'" Psalm 2:6-7

God's king would rule upon Mount Zion—one of the foremost hills in Jerusalem. At the same time, this king would have an even more important role. He wasn't simply a ruler, but he was the son of God! This would give him an amazing foundation. He would be the one who would have an unparalleled relationship with his Father (John 5:19). He would be taught by God morning by morning (Isaiah 50:4). He would be given the Holy Spirit without measure (John 3:34). Again, this same aspect of the Messiah, that he would be the son of God, was emphasized to David when God gave him a number of promises— but this time, there was an added element:

"When your days are fulfilled and you lie down with your fathers, I will raise up your offspring after you, who shall come from your body, and I will establish his kingdom...I will be to him a father, and he shall be to me a son." 2 Samuel 7:12, 14

While there was no specific time limit given to this prophecy, God promised that a ruler would come who would be His son. This is the same emphasis as the quote from Psalm 2. Yet perhaps even more striking—and most certainly more striking for David —was the fact that God told him that this king, Messiah, and son would be one of *his* descendants. The Messiah was to be one of David's offspring! What a privilege! And at the same time, what a message! This divine ruler wasn't going to be some type of "ethereal being" or some type of "spirit," but he was to be a *man*. As such, everything about his nature and his body would be just like his fellow men. In writing to the Hebrews, the apostle expressed this powerful message:

"Therefore he had to be made like his brothers in every respect, so that he might become a merciful and faithful high priest in the service of God, to make propitiation for the sins of the people." Hebrews 2:17

The son of God also *had* to be *the son of man*. He *had* to be part of humanity. He *had* to share our nature. In every respect, he was made "like his brothers." The emphatic writing of the apostle is hard to miss—and it almost seems to bring about an inevitable conclusion about the birth of the Lord. And thus God manifestation further changes the way in which we see the Lord Jesus.

Unlike what may be so often taught, when was the beginning of the Lord's life? Did he first exist in heaven with his Father, and then come down to earth and become a man? Or is it possible that, just like the rest of "his brothers," his life began with his birth?

Chapter 29 - Like You and Me

Have you ever just stopped and thought about Jesus? It can sometimes be difficult—our lives are filled with so many other things—but the benefits far outweigh the cost. As mentioned in the last chapter, when we think about Jesus, we realize that he was the son of God, yet also the son of man. In taking these few moments to set our minds on greater things and in lifting our eyes to Jesus, let us just consider the actual implications of this idea.

Sometimes in thinking on the Master's divine origin, we tend to miss this fact. We think about his greatness and we think about his exaltation to glory—but we don't often think about what it means for him to be a man (Acts 2:22, 1 Timothy 2:5). As a man—just like you and me—the Lord Jesus had to grow up and *learn* what it meant to truly serve God. At first, this suggestion may seem to be slightly profane; nevertheless, Scripture almost seeks to emphasize this point. Just after the story of the Lord being left in the temple by his parents, the divine narrative says:

"And Jesus increased in wisdom and in stature and in favor with God and man." Luke 2:52

Have you ever thought about Jesus increasing in *wisdom*? It might not at first seem possible, but in recognizing that Jesus was a man, just like us, it begins to make sense. As he grew from childhood to manhood, the Lord Jesus gained wisdom! He learned, just as we do! Unlike some of the common doctrines that teach that Christ always existed, or that he was all-knowing from the very beginning of time, Scripture plainly states that he grew in wisdom. Again, the same thing is said in the epistle to the Hebrews:

"Although he was a son, he learned obedience through what he suffered." Hebrews 5:8

Though Jesus was the son of God—and that fact is also not meant to be overlooked—he *learned* obedience! He was not all-knowing! While being son of God, he was also son of man. Just like us, he was born; just like us, he had to learn.

The implications behind this are incredible. The Savior of the world isn't some distant being who has never experienced our joys, sorrows, and pain. He isn't someone that is removed from our lives and our troubles. Just like you and me, he had to learn obedience. He understands the frustrations of fighting against sin. He understands the struggle of resisting temptation.

God manifestation isn't just an obscure doctrine for theologians to discuss. It is a doctrine that strikes deep at the heart of our relationship with the Lord Jesus Christ—it shows us that he *understands* that life is painful.

And yet, the writer to the Hebrews shows that this humanity and learning through suffering *perfected* the

Lord, allowing him to provide salvation for all of those who try to follow him:

"And being made perfect, he became the source of eternal salvation to all who obey him." Hebrews 5:9

He overcame and was changed—he was *made perfect* after his resurrection. Complete perfection, or glorious immortality, was something that had to be given to the Lord Jesus; as noted previously, it was not something that he had inherently. And thus, after his flesh was put to death, he was raised from the dead and made immortal—paving the way for "all who obey him." The apostle Paul wrote similarly about this change to the believers in Colossae. Note specifically the way that he described it:

"He is the image of the invisible God, the firstborn of all creation." Colossians 1:15

Often this verse is used to support the idea that Christ has existed from the beginning of time—and the term "firstborn of all creation" reads that way. But in fact, the apostle seems to have something else in mind—something that follows the same line of reasoning as Hebrews. Consider how this term is restated just a few verses later:

"And he is the head of the body, the church. He is the beginning, the firstborn from the dead, that in everything he might be preeminent." Colossians 1:18

Do you see the change? First Paul referred to Christ as "the firstborn of all creation," and shortly thereafter, he defined his term as "the firstborn from the dead."

In other words, Christ's role as the "beginning of creation" (Revelation 3:14) isn't because he existed before the physical world existed—it is because he was the *firstborn from the dead*. He was the first to be resurrected and given immortality.

But how does this connect to us?

Think about the word that Paul used: *firstborn*.

If there is a firstborn, what does that imply?

Just as Hebrews explained that Christ suffered and paved the way for those who would obey him, Paul asserted that Christ was the *firstborn* from the dead—implying that others would come after him.

Christ's humanity, his death, and his resurrection, are the model for us. He suffered, like us. He died, as we will. And yet, he was resurrected—as we hope to be.

In all these things, Christ was like us, so that he could be *our example.*

The Lord Jesus Christ is meant to be our inspiration. The teaching that Jesus existed before he was born takes away from that—because it claims that he possessed immortality before his birth. He couldn't have learned, he couldn't have died, he couldn't have been raised to be given immortality. He couldn't have been the *firstborn* from the dead.

Chapter 30 - The New Creation

In the last couple of chapters, we've seen that the Lord Jesus was like us and that this allowed him to be our example.

In considering that idea, we noted that Paul referred to him as "the firstborn of all creation" and then later "the firstborn from the dead."

And yet, why was it that the apostle chose to parallel these two phrases? How can being the "firstborn of all creation" be the same as being "the firstborn from the dead"?

Throughout the New Testament letters, the writers wrote about a *new creation*. Essentially, they explained that the Lord Jesus made a *second* creation possible. This wasn't a physical creation, like the creation of the trees and rocks and animals that was recorded in Genesis—instead, it was a *spiritual* creation, or one that began in the heart. Just notice the way that the apostle Paul uses the phrase:

"Therefore, if anyone is in Christ, he is a new creation. The old has passed away; behold, the new has come." 2 Corinthians 5:17

In Christ, we are part of a new creation (see also Galatians 6:14-15, Ephesians 2:10, and Ephesians 4:22-24)! Our old selves and our way of thinking have been crucified to the cross, and we walk forward as a new man. Through the work of the Master, a second creation has begun—a creation which begins, not at the physical creation of the world, but in the heart of each individual as they give up their old lives and resolve to live for God. Thus, Jesus is the means by which this new creation can exist; in this way, he is truly the "beginning of the creation." He wasn't created before the universe and before the creation in Genesis. He was the beginning of the *new* creation— the beginning of this second creation.

In his first epistle to the Corinthians, the apostle Paul again elaborated on this concept:

"Thus it is written, 'The first man Adam became a living being'; the last Adam became a life-giving spirit. But it is not the spiritual that is first but the natural, and then the spiritual." 1 Corinthians 15:45-46

The natural always comes first—the natural creation came before the spiritual creation. With both of these creations, there was a beginning. The first began with Adam. He was the first man ever created, and thus, he began the physical creation of mankind. Yet for the new creation there was another "Adam"—an Adam who was "life-giving." Who else could this be but the Lord Jesus? Over and over in Scripture, he explains that life can only come through him (John 10:10; John 14:6). He was the "last Adam"—the first man in this new creation. In this way, he truly was the *beginning* of the creation of God; not the beginning of the *physical* creation, but the beginning of the *spiritual* creation.

By following him and by crucifying our old way of thinking, we too can be part of this new creation. We can be renewed and recreated by God. We can find life in the Lord Jesus. This begins now, but ultimately, finds its full fulfillment when we are changed—when this mortal body puts on immortality and this perishable puts on the imperishable (1 Corinthians 15:53-54). We will be changed. We will be like him (1 John 3:2).

But for now, before we are physically changed, we must attempt to live as a new creation *today*. The decision is left up to us. Will we continue to live our lives for the present world, or will we join the firstborn of all creation—waiting for the day when not only our minds will be renewed, but all things, including this physical world, will be made new (Revelation 21:5)?

God manifestation is not simply an academic doctrine—it affects how we live *today*.

Section 5
The Cross

Chapter 31 - For God So Loved the World

John 3:16 is perhaps the most famous verse in all of Scripture: "For God so loved the world, that he gave his only Son, that whoever believes in him should not perish but have eternal life." In this verse is captured one of the great purposes of God with His son. In this declaration is the hope that comes through the Lord Jesus Christ. In this statement is a testimony to God's steadfast love. We see these words written on signs outside of churches, printed on pamphlets handed out by missionaries, and sometimes on bumper stickers. The verse is simple, and so is its message—but when we see it placarded before us, do we ever really take the time to think about it? Are we ever struck with awe when we realize what this verse *really* means? Do we fall down before the Father when we recognize that this verse means that *God loves us?*

The One who formed the seas, whose words caused the dry land to appear—He loves us. The One who could separate the light from the darkness, and who could give life to something that had long been dead —He loves us. He loves you. It isn't simply a trite phrase that we hear every day from Sunday school teachers or from people who use God's love almost as a catchphrase. It's a truth. God loved you so much, that He gave His son so that you could live forever with Him. Time and again, this is Scripture's message about the death of Christ:

"But God shows his love for us in that while we were still sinners, Christ died for us." Romans 5:8

"In this the love of God was made manifest among us, that God sent his only Son into the world, so that we might live through him. In this is love, not that we have loved God but that he loved us." 1 John 4:9-10

Sometimes you may have heard various people talk about the "atonement"—or the way in which sinful man can return to God—and the subject can get confusing because they use complex words or try to push their ideas about it. Sometimes they talk about an angry God whose wrath needed to be pacified by the death of His son on the cross. Sometimes they speak about the Lord Jesus being *punished* on the cross by his furious Father. Scripture knows nothing of that God. Rather, the essence of the atonement is found in that famous verse; God so loved the world that He gave His only son. That's the foundation of the atonement. The atonement was God's way of bringing fallen humanity back to a relationship with Himself—because He loved us! It wasn't about God's anger. It wasn't about God being appeased. It was about God's *love.*

As we take the time in these next few chapters to look at the atonement and the way in which we can be brought back to God, let us remember the foundation of it. God sent His son because *He loved us.*

Chapter 32 - Justice and Righteousness

Have you ever wondered how the cross could possibly be an act of love? It all seems too brutal and perhaps even barbaric.

Yet, as we saw in the last chapter, Scripture is adamant that the atonement is all about God's love for us. How could that be? How could the death of the son of God show God's love for you, for me, and for Jesus?

Many have attempted to answer this question with the statement, "Jesus died in my place," or "Jesus took my place." They state that we were supposed to die for our sins, but Jesus died instead of us. Along with these statements they advance verses like "he was wounded for our transgressions" (Isaiah 53:5), or he "bore our sins in his body" (1 Peter 2:24). And, at first glance, they would appear to be right. A cursory reading of these passages sound as though the Lord Jesus had our sins put upon him when he was on the cross—and he was punished for those. The Master took our place by bearing our very sins—the worst of them all—endured God's wrath and anger for those sins, and then perished upon the cross, suffering the very punishment which we deserved, *instead of us.* Such is a fairly common understanding of the cross.

While this teaching may at first sound plausible and true, there is a sizable issue with it—just consider this: can an angry and vengeful God who punishes His innocent son in the place of sinners *really* be called *love?* Just try to imagine what that would mean in today's society. It would almost be like a father who had two sons, one who was rebellious and disobedient, and one who always did what he was asked. Yet every time the rebellious son transgressed his father's commands, the father, in his wrath and anger, punished the innocent one for the crimes of the guilty—supposedly because he loved the guilty son and wanted him to live in liberty! It would be fairly outrageous!

Is that the kind of God that we worship? Is He really a God who punished His innocent son for our crimes? Does "he was wounded for our transgressions" mean that he took our place—that he died *instead* of us?

I'd like to suggest that the answer to all three of these questions *must* be a resounding "no." This may seem like a strong statement—but just consider what follows. The God of Scripture is *always* described as a God of justice and righteousness. Below are two passages that describe Him:

"The Rock, his work is perfect, for all his ways are justice. A God of faithfulness and without iniquity, just and upright is he." Deuteronomy 32:4

"And there is no other god besides me, a righteous God and a Savior; there is none besides me." Isaiah 45:21

God is a God of justice and righteousness (cp. Ezra 9:15; Daniel 9:14; Zephaniah 3:5). He will not punish the innocent for the sins of the guilty—so would he really allow his Son to die in the place of sinners? This idea would seem to fly in the face of justice and righteousness. In fact, this type of action is even condemned in the book of Proverbs:

"He who justifies the wicked and he who condemns the righteous are both alike an abomination to the Lord." Proverbs 17:15

What man was more righteous than the Lord Jesus Christ? Yet so often his crucifixion is understood to be the condemnation of the righteous for the justification of the wicked—such action, according to Proverbs, is an abomination to God! To simply take away the sins of the wicked and place them on the innocent son of God would absolutely violate God's justice. Even more, not only would it violate God's justice, but it would be a twisted understanding of love. How could the crucifixion *really* be about God's love if it truly meant that Jesus died instead of sinners?

It couldn't. It *absolutely* couldn't.

But then what did it all mean? If Jesus *didn't* die in our place, then why did he die? If God didn't punish Christ on the cross and make him pay for our sins, then what was the crucifixion all about?

Chapter 33 - Declaring Righteousness

Scripture is adamant that the Lord Jesus' death was an act of God's love. It was an act of love towards a population of mankind which was dying and had no other hope.

Yet, it was an act of love which is so often misunderstood. Over and over it is advanced from the pulpits and platforms that the Master gave his life on the cross because he *endured God's wrath for our sins*. According to those who stand for this idea, he suffered the punishment that we deserved for our sins, allowing us to go free.

However, as we saw in the last chapter, something about this idea just doesn't fit. God is a God of righteousness and justice—those two attributes are major parts of His character, and punishing an innocent man for the guilt of others really has nothing to do with justice or righteousness. Even more, not only does God emphasize that He places such a great importance on justice and righteousness, in the book of Romans, the apostle Paul wrote that Christ's death on the cross was in itself *a declaration of God's righteousness*:

"For all have sinned and fall short of the glory of God, and are justified by his grace as a gift, through the redemption that is in Christ Jesus, whom God put forward as a propitiation by his blood, to be received by faith. This was to show God's righteousness, because in his divine forbearance he had passed over former sins." Romans 3:23-25

Somehow, the cross of Christ demonstrated God's righteousness—not because an angry God punished His innocent son, but because a God of love showed that He was just. Yet exactly *how* did He do this through requiring His son to die on a cross?

One of the major things about Christ that Scripture emphasizes is that he came *as a man.* He was the son of God, yet he was human. He thought like we think, he had emotions as we do, and he felt temptation like we do. Over and over the Scriptural record explains this (Galatians 4:4; Hebrews 2:14, 17)—and in doing so, also explains *why* this fleshly nature was so essential:

"For God has done what the law, weakened by the flesh, could not do. By sending his own Son in the likeness of sinful flesh and for sin, he condemned sin in the flesh." Romans 8:3

Jesus' death on the cross *condemned sin!* This was how it declared God's righteousness! The Lord Jesus lived his life in utter and complete innocence, never sinning—yet at the end of his life, he still *willingly* submitted to death because he acknowledged *that everyone must fight the mental war against sin and flesh must die.* Our flesh is the root of sin. It isn't sinful in itself—but sin begins in our fleshly nature and our fleshly hearts (Jeremiah 17:9; Mark 7:21-23). The Lord Jesus declared that God was righteous by submitting to the death on the cross though he had never committed sin—in doing so, he showed that God's condemnation of our fleshly nature to death was *right*. He declared God *righteous*.

Thus, the Lord's death openly proclaimed that God's ways and precepts were just. Flesh must die.

And so we can see how Christ's death declared God to be righteous—but where exactly does love fit into all of this? And where do we fit? How can the Lord's death affect us?

Chapter 34 - Giving Your Life

Because we're human, we're dying.

Eventually, all of us will take our last breath. From there, we'll turn back into the dust from which we are made. As God said to Adam, "for you are dust, and to dust you shall return" (Genesis 3:19). All throughout Scripture, faithful men and women of old have recognized this. In fact, King David described death as a state in which we have no consciousness (Psalm 6:5). Wise King Solomon wrote similar words, stating that "the living know that they will die, but the dead know nothing" (Ecclesiastes 9:5). The sons of Korah, a group of faithful brethren who wrote a few of the psalms, equated the end of our lives to the end of an animal's life:

"Man in his pomp yet without understanding is like the beasts that perish." Psalm 49:20

In death, mankind is just like the animals. Our mighty intentions perish, our thoughts disappear, and all our desires fade away (Psalm 146:3-4). We cannot praise God and we cannot curse him. Everything is gone and everything is over. This is an indisputable truth of Scripture. When we die, *we are dead*—and that death is just and right. All of us have sinned, and as a result, we all deserve death (Romans 3:23; Romans 6:23).

But it doesn't have to be that way—and that's the *love* of the atonement.

In the last few chapters, we've spent our time looking at God's righteousness. We've sought to understand the meaning behind the atonement, and we've seen that in the Lord's sacrifice, God's righteousness was declared. Nevertheless, one of the primary focuses of the cross was to show God's love—and in chapter after chapter, we acknowledged that the atonement was a *major* act of God's love, but we've yet to touch on *how* it was such.

It wasn't an act of love because Christ took our punishment—there's no justice in that. Rather, it was an act of love because it showed us *how* to escape the death sentence that was given to all mankind. As Jesus hung on the cross, he was an example to us— not a substitute. In his death, he was *showing us what we needed to do:*

"For to this you have been called, because Christ also suffered for you, leaving you an example, so that you might follow in his steps." 1 Peter 2:21

Christ's sacrifice showed us the path to life—and that path was bound up in "death." As he explained to his disciples, in order to truly find life, one must be willing to give up the life that they live now by choosing God's will over their own:

"And calling the crowd to him with his disciples, he said to them, "If anyone would come after me, let him deny himself and take up his cross and follow me. For whoever would save his life will lose it, but whoever loses his life for my sake and the gospel's will save it." Mark 8:34-35

True life can only be found in giving ours away. We have been called to pick up our own cross and follow the Lord to Calvary. Truly, some have been called to literally give up their lives for the gospel's sake, but for many of us, this giving of our lives is something that takes place every day. It's in the choice that we make when we decide what type of activity we'll do in our free time. It's in the group of people with whom we decide to spend our time and the types of things that we do with them. It's in the opportunities and decisions that present themselves to us each day.

Will we choose to die to sin and live for God? Or will we give in to our sinful nature and allow that part of us to continue to live on?

God, in an amazing outpouring of love, gave His son Jesus so that you could have life. In his death, Christ powerfully showed what choice we *should* make. May we be moved by that example. Indeed, if that doesn't move us, then what will?

Chapter 35 - Dying with Christ

Do you ever feel overwhelmed when you consider the Lord Jesus? He never sinned; never once gave into envy or pride. He was completely and entirely perfect—even to the point of giving up his life in a gift of obedience to his Father and love to the world. How could we ever follow in the steps of such a man? How could we ever even attempt to do the same things which he did?

Yet as Christ spoke to the multitude, his words were unyielding:

"Whoever does not bear his own cross and come after me cannot be my disciple." Luke 14:27

Looking past even his daily struggles against sin, the Master proclaimed his ultimate demonstration of love. He was going to give his life on a cross. Yet as he spoke about this sacrifice, his thoughts didn't end with his own offering—the call went straight out to all of those who would seek to follow him.

Anyone who wants to follow the Lord Jesus must give up their life by living for God. We saw this in the last chapter. The power of the atonement is that it calls us, not simply to stand in awe of what the Master did, but to do the same ourselves. We must follow him to Calvary. We must pick up our own cross and stumble along that dusty road, just as he did. If we don't, the Lord's words are clear—we cannot be his disciple.

If considering the Lord didn't overwhelm us before, perhaps that's because we hadn't considered this calling. True Christians are those who are motivated by the love demonstrated in the cross to follow the Lord's footsteps (2 Corinthians 5:14-15).

But mercifully, the giving of our lives can be different to the way in which the Lord gave up his. Each day, just as he did, we are called to give up our own pleasures and serve the Father. Nevertheless, our cross doesn't have to be literal. Instead, when we choose to die with the Lord Jesus, we can be baptized into his name. The immersion in the water and subsequent raising up symbolize both a death and resurrection—such was the interpretation given to the act by the apostle Paul:

"Do you not know that all of us who have been baptized into Christ Jesus were baptized into his death? We were buried therefore with him by baptism into death, in order that, just as Christ was raised from the dead by the glory of the Father, we too might walk in newness of life." Romans 6:3-4

This is how we die with the Lord Jesus. We are baptized into his death, and as we come up out of the water, we seek to live in "newness of life." We make new choices and we set our focus on better things— but not only that, we also are given a hope for the future. As the apostle went on to say, if we have truly died with Christ, then we believe that just as Jesus was raised up from the dead, eventually, the same thing will happen to us:

"Now if we have died with Christ, we believe that we will also live with him. We know that Christ, being raised from the dead, will never die again; death no longer has dominion over him." Romans 6:8-9

If we die with Christ—being baptized into him and then seeking to enact that symbolic death by walking in "newness of life"—then we have the hope that one day, just as he was raised from the dead, we too will be raised up again to life in the future age.

Such is the hope of the Biblical believer.

Chapter 36 - Resurrection to Life

For centuries and millennia, mankind has sought for life after death.

But for those who put their trust in the Holy Scriptures, truly, there is only one way:

"Jesus said to him, "I am the way, and the truth, and the life. No one comes to the Father except through me." John 14:6

Though religion after religion may espouse their own path to salvation, life after death can only be found in the Lord Jesus Christ. He is the life—and following him, through his death, resurrection, and change of nature is what can bring this life.

As we've seen in the past articles, the Lord Jesus is our example. We've been called to "die with him"—to perform a symbolic death and resurrection in baptism. Then, throughout our lives, we seek to live anew.

Yet baptism is simply symbolic. It is an acknowledgment of our desire to crucify our sin-prone nature and to live to God. Crucifixion isn't something we are expected to do literally (thankfully!)—but God does expect us to fight our sinful desires, put them to death and change the way we live. God want us to become more like Jesus by treating people with love, kindness, mercy and patience, and trusting whatever the Lord brings into our lives. As Paul explains:

"Put to death therefore what is earthly in you: sexual immorality, impurity, passion, evil desire, and covetousness, which is idolatry. On account of these the wrath of God is coming. In these you too once walked, when you were living in them. But now you must put them all away: anger, wrath, malice, slander, and obscene talk from your mouth. Do not lie to one another, seeing that you have put off the old self with its practices and have put on the new self, which is being renewed in knowledge after the image of its creator." Colossians 3:5-10

When we are baptized, we act out this desire to be changed, and we show our God our willingness and desire to follow His son. Therefore, in His mercy, the Father pledges that those who seek to follow the Lord in symbol and action, will one day follow the Lord in resurrection and immortality. Whereas they put to death the old man *in symbol*, and tried throughout their lives to live for God, one day, God will do for them that which they could never do for themselves:

"For if we have been united with him in a death like his, we shall certainly be united with him in a resurrection like his." Romans 6:5

God will give them life. In dying with the Lord in symbol at baptism, they will be raised with the Lord in reality. This is the secret of immortality. When the Lord Jesus returns to this earth, those who have died with him will follow the pattern which he set—they will be raised to life:

"For the Lord himself will descend from heaven with a cry of command, with the voice of an archangel, and with the sound of the trumpet of God. And the dead in Christ will rise." 1 Thessalonians 4:16

The dead in Christ will rise. It's as simple as that. Though men have devoted years of their lives to their quest for immortality, the answer is found in the Lord Jesus and His Father. Eternal life will be given at the resurrection. It isn't something that we have innately (Romans 2:7; 1 Corinthians 15:53). We don't have a soul that lives on after death (Psalm 49:12, 20; Ecclesiastes 3:18-21). Instead, life is given at the return of the Lord, and with that life comes a change in our nature (1 Corinthians 15:50-51; Philippians 3:21):

"We know that when he appears we shall be like him, because we shall see him as he is." 1 John 3:2

We shall be like him. No longer will we be sinful and dying creatures. Instead, we will be made like the Lord Jesus Christ. We will be partakers of the divine nature (2 Peter 1:4).

And truly, *that* is the love of the atonement. Through the death and resurrection of the Lord Jesus Christ, we have been given an example of the way to our God. We must follow him in baptism, and by God's grace, we will follow him in his resurrection.

But there is one final event that must take place between the resurrection and the giving of life: the judgment seat of the Lord Jesus.

Chapter 37 - Judgment

None of us want to be judged. By our very nature, that's just how we feel. Many people claim that they won't judge someone else—in relation to their way of life or their decisions—specifically because they don't want that person to turn the judgment around and start judging them!

Nevertheless, with God, there will be a judgment day for those who have heard and understood His message. It won't be for everyone—just those who know the gospel. As we have mentioned in previous chapters, for many people who haven't ever heard the good news, they live and then they turn back to the dust, just like the animals (Genesis 3:19). As it was written in the psalms:

"Man in his pomp yet without understanding is like the beasts that perish." Psalm 49:20

Though a man might have filled his life with achievements and glory, if he didn't have an understanding of the gospel, he is like the beasts that perish. Just like the animals, he will return to the dust. This judgment isn't for everyone—only for those who have been exposed to the Word and who have understood its message (see John 12:48).

For those of us, though, who have been given a knowledge of the true gospel message, judgment isn't something that needs to be feared. Indeed, it will be a day in which some are condemned—but it will also be a day in which *true life* or *immortality* is finally given to those who believed! It can be a day that is exciting! The Lord will come, his voice will open the graves, and the judgment will commence. Those who, through their belief have dedicated their lives to doing good, will be given true life. Those who have, through their disbelief, dedicated their lives to doing evil, will be condemned:

"Do not marvel at this, for an hour is coming when all who are in the tombs will hear his voice and come out, those who have done good to the resurrection of life, and those who have done evil to the resurrection of judgment." John 5:28-29

Those in the graves will hear the Lord's voice. They will be resurrected, and they will be judged. Some will go to the right, and be given eternal life in God's kingdom (Matthew 25:34). Others, tragically, will go to the left, where they will be condemned (Matthew 25:41). This isn't meant to scare us—but it's meant to remind us that when we look at the Bible, we aren't looking at just a trivial matter. This is life and death. It could be the best day of our lives, or it could be the worst.

The atonement is a message of love—and it is a message of hope. Those who give their lives over to the Father will enter into His family and will be given the opportunity to live forever with Him. Death will not conquer them. Yet, at the same time, the atonement is also a sobering message. It isn't simply a free card to go and live however we want. Once we hear the message, we have to respond.

Because of love, a man died on a hill outside of Jerusalem—and now, knowing those things, and knowing that our God is watching for our response, what choice will we make?

Will we follow the steps of the Lord through baptism? Will we continue to seek truth? Or will we merely go on with life, unmoved by the power of the atonement?

The choice is ours—but, let it not be forgotten that, while our God is a God of love and mercy, and while He *longs* to give us life, He won't forget what choice we choose to make.

Let us, then, strive to make the right choice, and allow the power of Christ's atonement to soften our hardened hearts.

Chapter 38 - The Kingdom

And so we've come full circle. But that's the beautiful thing about the gospel—it's all interlinked and woven together. And it all makes sense. Just like God's truth should.

So just take a moment to remind yourself of the hope of all of this.

Someday, the Lord Jesus will come again. There will be no more waiting, there will be no more wondering. The Master will have returned. And on that day, he will gather together his own:

"When the Son of Man comes in his glory, and all of the angels with him, then he will set on his glorious throne. Before him will be gathered all the nations, and he will separate people one from another as a shepherd separates the sheep from the goats. And he will place the sheep on his right, but the goats on the left." Matthew 25:31-33

When the Lord returns, he will gather his followers together (Matthew 13:47-50). Then, they will stand before him as he issues the judgment. Some will walk to the right and some will walk to the left. We've already spent some time considering what that will all be like. But now, we want to consider what comes after—particularly for those on the right:

"Then the King will say to those on his right, 'Come, you who are blessed by my Father, inherit the kingdom prepared for you from the foundation of the world.'" Matthew 25:34

This is the hope offered to those who walk in faith. "Come...inherit the kingdom." Can you imagine hearing those words? What will it be like? What will you say? By God's grace, may these be the words that we hear from the mouth of the Master.

The kingdom of God is the hope offered in Scripture. It's a picture of a renewed world—a world which will be filled with righteousness and peace. The Lord Jesus described it as he taught his disciples how to pray:

"Your kingdom come, your will be done, on earth as it is in heaven." Matthew 6:10

This was such an essential element of their faith, that the Lord Jesus wanted his disciples to pray for it. He wanted them to yearn for it. The kingdom was the time when man's will would no longer be done on earth. It was the time when God's will would fill the mountains and the valleys. Rather than corruption, society would be filled with righteousness.

Have you ever longed for world peace? That's the kingdom of God! Just try to imagine a world in which lying and cheating are virtually nonexistent. Try to imagine a world where there is no violence. In the book of Isaiah, the prophet explained what that time will be like—all of the nations will get rid of their weapons because they won't need them any longer!

"It shall come to pass in the latter days that the mountain of the house of the LORD shall be established as the highest of the mountains, and shall be lifted up above the hills...He shall judge between the nations, and shall decide disputes for many peoples; and they shall beat their swords into plowshares, and their spears into pruning hooks; nation shall not lift up sword against nation, neither shall they learn war anymore." Isaiah 2:2, 4

This is the hope that is offered to us. God doesn't promise heaven. Instead, He offers a resurrection—a conquering of the grave—and an offer to live forever in His kingdom, when all the earth will be filled with His glory (Numbers 14:21). This was the purpose of the atonement. The Lord Jesus died so that we could have this offer.

Really, the question is, will we take it?

Made in the USA
Middletown, DE
03 June 2023

31670736R00083